THE POET'S PEN

THE POET'S PEN
Writing Poetry with Middle and High School Students

BETTY BONHAM LIES

Illustrated by
Brian Lies

Teacher Ideas Press
An Imprint of Greenwood Publishing Group
361 Hanover Street
Portsmouth, New Hampshire
1993

For Tom
Sine Quo Non

TEACHER IDEAS PRESS
An Imprint of Greenwood Publishing Group
361 Hanover Street
Portsmouth, NH 03801
1-800-225-5800
www.teacherideaspress.com

Library of Congress Cataloging-in-Publication Data

Lies, Betty Bonham.
    The poet's pen : writing poetry with middle and high school students / Betty Bonham Lies ; illustrated by Brian Lies.
    xvi, 201 p. 17x25 cm.
    Includes bibliographical references and index.
    ISBN 1-56308-111-3
    1. Poetry--Study and Teaching (Secondary)   I. Title.
PN1101.L54   1993
808.1'0712--dc20   93-18806
                                              CIP

Docutech T & C 2004

And as imagination bodies forth
The forms of things unknown, the poet's pen
Turns them to shapes, and gives to airy nothing
A local habitation and a name.

—William Shakespeare,
A Midsummer Night's Dream

Contents

Preface

*Poetry tells us the stories of the
soul in its earthly adventure.*

— Stanley Kunitz

On Monday, Jill wrote:

> In a society were one person as so much control to shoot and kill
> were the police in the first didnt fireback at him for the reason
> that most police offercers are unarmered because of the gun laws
> are so strict were as a police offericer doesnt carry a gun to
> protect themselves and the people but were as an single man can
> get a rifle, a hand gun, and a granade.

On Tuesday, she wrote:

> Love is a china-pink rose
> that glimmers in the night
> and leaves fragrances of pain.

This book originated in two observations I made after I began to have
students in my English classes write poetry regularly throughout the school year.

The first observation, which will come as no surprise to teachers who have
worked with poetry in the classroom, was that many of my best poets were to be
found among the students traditionally labeled the weakest. Expository writing
by these students is sometimes appalling, but in poetry they may create compelling images and metaphors, use language in both creative and precise ways,
play with words and ideas, and express their thoughts freely. At the same time,
some of my students who were at the top of their classes wrote rather pedestrian
and stilted poetry.

A common explanation for the phenomenon of high poetic achievement
among traditionally lower-ranked students is that the "better" students are too
worried about correctness, grades, and what they think the teacher wants to be
free in creative assignments. I believe there is truth in this explanation. But I
began to wonder whether there might be another reason: Perhaps it happens, at

least partly, because the "less good" students are different kinds of learners, doomed to be labeled "less good" *because* they learn differently, and their learning styles are not always identified and encouraged in school. I know that with the positive stimulation of having their voices heard and their writing praised, these poets in my classroom perked up, gained self-confidence, and began to view themselves differently as English students. And, in fact, they became better students.

My second observation, somewhat more surprising to me at the time, was the startling improvement in expository writing among all my students who were writing poetry regularly. One day in the spring, after reading the novel *1984*, my tenth-grade class read aloud their responses to the assignment "Describe your own Room 101." I was so overwhelmed by the power of their writing that when my next class came into the room, I couldn't even remember what they were studying. I had momentarily ceased to be teacher and was responding to the writing only as a deeply affected reader. And that instance was just one of several in which these students' expository writing was unusually compelling. Why, I wondered, did poetry writing seem to lead to such powerful prose? Those students hadn't been better writers in the fall than any other tenth-grade class I have taught. Nor had they written more than previous classes; in fact, in terms of sheer volume of words, they had produced less.

I began to ask myself what had happened and how I could use this discovery to help all my students write more fluently, freshly, and authentically. I decided to embark on a study based on both classroom experimentation and theoretical research to answer those questions. *The Poet's Pen* is the result of my investigation of why and how to teach poetry writing and to integrate it into the rest of the secondary school curriculum instead of isolating it in creative writing electives or occasional self-contained units within an English class.

I believe similarities exist between the best expository and creative writing: Both surprise the reader with new ideas and startle with aptness of expression; both make the reader sit up and notice the familiar in a new way; both use figurative language, vivid images, and precise words; and both reveal the voice and thoughts of the writer. Using the two kinds of writing in combination—in all subject areas—does, I am convinced, help students become both better writers and better learners. When I began to study this relationship, I expected to discover something about the connections between right- and left-brain functions. But as I dug into psychology texts and talked with psychology professors, I learned that too little is known about how the brain works to reach any scientific conclusion about the interaction of imagination and reason. And yet, after researching and observing that interaction, I became even more convinced that making the connection is terribly important for students.

What I do know from my academic research and classroom experience is that poetry writing works. Students whose imaginative capacities are sparked and fanned into flame, who experiment with new ways of using language, and who begin to view life through a poetic lens increase their comfort and facility with all kinds of writing—and the effect of poetry writing goes further. It helps writers see and understand the world in new ways; it makes them better learners. In addition, expressive writing is always a journey in self-discovery, an important step in the adolescent's task of developing a sense of self and of self-worth.

Jill knows perfectly well that her prose sentence doesn't say what she wants to say, and she is ashamed of it; in fact, it makes her feel she is a failure. But her metaphor about love clearly defines a feeling and shows that she has a real sensitivity to language. Shouldn't her success be built upon to help her develop her skills? Through poetry she not only has a chance to understand and articulate her own ideas; she also earns honest praise, and the resulting self-esteem makes her next attempt more promising.

Writing poetry can help not only the Jills in our classes. Very often the most academic students write lifeless, pedantic, or dull — although mechanically correct — prose, and they often find it difficult to free themselves of scholastic constraints in order to express their real thoughts and especially their feelings. Poetry works wonders for them, too.

Not all students will produce deathless poetry and prose, but that's not the point; rather, it is about stretching and learning. Still, just stand back and wait for the forms that emerge — the insights, discoveries, and wonderful language that we didn't know we had in us. You and your students will be shocked, amazed, and delighted by what comes forth when you pick up the poet's pen.

This book is for teachers. Its purpose is to encourage the teaching of poetry writing and to help you in your daily life by providing a storehouse of practical plans ready to use in the classroom. It is meant to convince the skeptical, encourage the convinced, and reassure the novice. For the teacher who has done little, if any, poetry writing with students, it offers detailed suggestions on getting started and working poetry into your curriculum; it describes some classroom-tested exercises and gives you ideas about constructing your own lessons and assignments. For the teacher who already works with poetry writing, it has new ideas to add to your own bag of tricks and provides you with support in arguing the case for poetry. And for those who aren't yet convinced that poetry writing is important for all students, the first chapter gives a rationale, based on academic and experiential research, for making poetry writing part of your curriculum.

In addition to the ideas for classroom lessons, exercises, and assignments (these assignments appear in italics because they are addressed to the student, not the teacher), I provide an annotated bibliography of other books you might find helpful allies in your venture, as well as a glossary of terms used in this book. And for your interest and inspiration, I include a number of poems written by my students in the last five years, during which I have tried out the ideas I describe here. These poems might serve to encourage your students as well as you.

I hope you will enjoy working with *The Poet's Pen*.

Acknowledgments

First, I wish to express my thanks for the inspiration and example of Lynn Powell, who raised my voice as a poet and whose visits to my classes gave me so many ideas and the confidence to expand poetry writing with my students. Craig Czury encouraged me as both poetry teacher and writer and helped me to publish.

This book would not have been written without the generous support of the Esther A. and Joseph Klingenstein Foundation, which sponsored my research during my year as a Klingenstein Fellow at Teachers College, Columbia University. Klingenstein Center Director Pearl R. Kane aided and cheered me on throughout the project and gave me much sage advice.

I am grateful to Geraldine R. Dodge Foundation Executive Director Scott McVay and Poetry Coordinator James Haba for their indefatigable work to "befriend poetry" and their sustained support of New Jersey poetry teachers and students through programs that include poets in the schools, workshops for teachers, and the Dodge Poetry Festival.

Thanks are also due to several colleagues who critiqued my manuscript in its early form: Christina Moustakis, English Department Head, Manhattan Friends School; Peter Herzberg, English Department Head, Dwight-Englewood School; John Mason, Dean of Faculty, Tilton School; and Dr. Barbara King-Shaver, English Supervisor, South Brunswick High School. My editors, Suzanne Barchers and Deborah Korte, have made the later stages seem a breeze.

Finally, I want to thank my family: Elaine, Brian, and Laurel, each of whom has given me something very special in the way of encouragement, and especially Tom, for constant support.

1 Why Teach Poetry Writing?

God guard me from those thoughts men think
in the mind alone;
He that sings a lasting song
Thinks in a marrow-bone.

—William Butler Yeats

As with the stereoscope, depth is better
achieved from looking from two points at
once.

— Jerome Bruner

Use your head!
Be reasonable!
Prove it!
Support with logical reasons!
Give me a rational explanation!
Tell me what you think, not what you feel!
Oh, you always have your head in the clouds!

Phrases like these ring through childhood—at home, on the playground, in the classroom—in our society, whose fundamental values are founded on a philosophy that considers logic and reason the highest human function. We value clear thinking, by which we mean logical thinking, while intuition is suspect as a basis for reaching a conclusion. Propositions are tested by how logical they are; we speak of irrationality as a sign of madness. The progress of society is measured by technological and economic advancement, and in support of efficient, rational progress, we have erected authoritarian structures in all our social institutions: government, industry, business, religion, and education.

Today this philosophy is being questioned in many quarters. Yet it is still institutionalized in the hierarchical structures of our middle and high schools, which organize the people in the system from superintendent to principal to department chair to teacher to student; in the division into departments and disciplines; in the scientifically planned and organized daily schedule; and in the way learning is traditionally structured in classrooms, with the teacher as an expositor who imparts information to students.

Many recent school reform proposals have called for an even deeper plunge into the technical-rational approach to education, citing standardized test scores to prove the need for stressing "the basics," emphasizing testable skills and competencies, making lists of facts that will confer "cultural literacy," or introducing the metaphor of school as business, run on the factory model, with students as the product.

For the most part, the curricula of secondary schools stress cognitive skills; although periodically there have been attempts to include the affective domain, in reality it is rarely given a high priority. Feeling, intuition, and imagination are denied as valid bases for curriculum design or pedagogical methods and often even seem to pose "a threat to stability and equilibrium."[1] Cognitively based achievement tests are still used as the primary evaluation of schools, students, and teaching. College admissions testing and Advanced Placement tests have done much to dictate college preparatory curriculum and methods. Under these pressures and the financial constraints schools find themselves facing, the arts and other areas that attempt to touch on less easily tested skills are shunted to the sidelines or eliminated entirely from school programs.

Yet when groups of teachers get together—in professional meetings or classes, at conferences and seminars—the statement "What we really need to do is get these kids' imaginations working" causes a stir of heartfelt agreement around the room.

As teachers, we know from classroom experience that there are as many types of learners as there are students in the room with us and that leaning too heavily on the testable, the objective, or the verifiable causes some students to turn school off. It doesn't surprise us when psychologist Howard Gardner identifies seven different types of intelligence.[2] It seems clear that a curriculum built on only two types of intellectual competence—the linguistic (verbal skills) and the logical (mathematical skills)—will shut out certain students from their best type of learning. What's more, we know that a classroom that operates only by conveying information from teacher to pupil encourages passive learning for most students.[3] Dependence on the teacher for learning factual information to be echoed back on a test results in a shallow and too soon forgotten grasp of the material.

So we look for ways to engage students in their education, to help them learn more than facts, think for themselves, ask provocative questions, and use their imaginative, creative, divergent, playful capacities as well as logical reasoning: in short, to become dynamic learners by using their entire range of mental energies.

Challenging the dominant rational pattern does not mean an attempt to institutionalize a different kind of one-dimensional education in our schools. As teachers, we know the power of using reason and imagination together to deepen learning. What we want to do is create curricula and classroom practices that engage both thinking and feeling, reason and imagination, to accommodate various learning styles. We do not have to take sides over different ways of thinking in "a battle between reason and feeling, rationality and irrationality, logic and impulse."[4] Rather, by considering those qualities as complementary intellectual functions, we might find ways to use them in combination throughout our schools to help all students achieve their best. As Maxine Greene puts it: "It is not a matter of rejecting the theoretical, the propositional, the analytical; nor is it a question of 'leaving out math.' The problem is to find ways of freeing students to become conscious of their various interpretive undertakings and to learn how to reflect upon the ways there are of ordering experience, of making the world."[5]

> *Rationalists, wearing square hats,*
> *Think, in square rooms,*
> *Looking at the floor,*
> *Looking at the ceiling.*
> *They confine themselves*
> *To right-angled triangles.*
> *If they tried rhomboids,*
> *Cones, waving lines, ellipses —*
> *As, for example, the ellipse of the half-moon —*
> *Rationalists would wear sombreros.*
>
> —Wallace Stevens

Let's prepare our students to be wearers of sombreros.

EXPOSITORY AND POETIC WRITING: ARE THEY POLES APART?

> *Only connect! Only connect the prose and*
> *the passion, and both will be exalted.*
>
> —E. M. Forster

More than twenty years ago, James Britton introduced the ideas that led to contemporary approaches to teaching writing, with his definition of different kinds of writing.[6] To Britton, writing begins in what he calls the "expressive" mode (the natural expression of the personality) and can move in two opposite directions: to the "transactional" (for the purpose of informing or persuading) or to the "poetic" (formed literary writing):

transactional ◄——————— expressive ——————► poetic

This should be seen as a continuum rather than a scale with two distinct and opposite poles; writing of various types falls on different points along the continuum.

Most American classrooms today focus on moving students toward the transactional or expository end of the continuum. The more concerned we become about the quality of student writing, the more we work on the essay, the proper construction of a paragraph, organizing ideas, and conveying information clearly. We assign and worry over critical analysis of literature, research papers, laboratory reports. Research has shown that from the earliest years, most classrooms require students to use linear exposition in talking, developing ideas, and writing, although many people express themselves more naturally in other modes. In spite of a recent increase in journal writing and reader response to literature, a majority of the writing demanded in schools is still transactional rather than expressive, and working on the poetic mode is a real rarity. Creative writing is often relegated to elective English classes, and poetry especially is considered a frill, only occasionally assigned even in the English classroom.

I would argue that to improve students' writing, we must help them extend their skills toward both ends of the writing continuum, enabling them to move freely between the various modes. While it is clear that the two extremes—expository writing and poetry—are very different from one another and have different purposes, it is not clear how different are the kinds of thinking that lead to the best expression in each mode. Although poetry may lie more in the realm of imagination, and logical discourse in the realm of reason, the two forms of expression have much in common. Both call for imagination and creativity to arrive at an original thought and to formulate that thought. For both, the writer must use reason to develop an idea in the appropriate form, to find details that support or illustrate the idea, and to express it in precise language. In both exposition and poetic writing, the subject matter and the writer's individual voice, knowledge, and experience work together to shape the structure and guide all the author's decisions.

Students often believe that poetry is an unreasoned, spontaneous spill of emotion, rising from an unknown impulse or inspiration, unchecked by thought. But, as Jacques Maritain writes, "Poetry cannot be reduced to a mere gushing forth of images unseparated from intelligence, any more than to a discursus of logical reason."[7] Look at what some poets have said about the need for tempering poetic insight with deliberate thought:

T. S. Eliot:	There is a great deal, in the writing of poetry, which must be conscious and deliberate.
Novalis:	It is impossible for the poet to be too cool, too collected.
Achim von Arnim:	There has never been a poet without passion. But it is not passion which makes the poet. No poet has ever done lasting work in the instant when he was dominated by passion.
Charles Baudelaire:	Everything that is beautiful and noble is the result of reason and calculation.

At the same time, the best discourses of logical reason are, in many ways, poetic. Figurative language, original and striking phrasing, precise and interesting words, and imagery all bring expository writing to life and increase its power to instruct or persuade.

Significant implications for teaching writing ensue from a new look at the relationship between reason and imagination. Peter Elbow defines two kinds of thinking: "first-order," which is intuitive and creative, and "second-order," which is conscious, direct, and controlled; he suggests that moving back and forth between the two enriches them both. "Second-order thinking often brings out people's worst thinking. 'Thinking carefully' means trying to examine your thinking while using it too.... This is one of the main reasons why shrewd and sensible students often write essays asserting things they don't really believe and defending them with wooden reasoning.... First-order thinking, on the other hand, often heightens intelligence." If we do not use both intuitive thinking to generate ideas and insights and logical thinking to criticize and impose structure, Elbow suggests, "we end up with disciplined critical thinking and uncensored creative thinking dug into opposed trenches with their guns trained on each other. If we would see clearly how it really is with thinking and writing, we would see that ... the more first-order thinking, the more second-order thinking; the more generative uncensored writing, the more critical revision; and vice versa."[8]

Developing each kind of thinking and writing enhances the development of the other: Transactional or expository prose becomes stronger when the imagination is also in play; poetic expression is sharpened when it is examined rationally. We could help students improve all their writing by making better use of this mutually reinforcing dialectic.

POETRY AS MEANING MAKER

Poetry may make us see the world afresh, or some new part of it. It may make us from time to time a little more aware of the deeper, unnamed feelings to which we rarely penetrate.

—T. S. Eliot

The Search for Meaning

A ... poet is a discoverer, rather than an inventor.

— Jorge Luis Borges

One of the developmental tasks growing children face is to make meaning of the world around them. That task has become increasingly difficult in our era of cultural and moral relativism, lack of agreement on basic values, and a growing sense of helplessness in the face of world problems that seem out of an individual's control.

Many psychologists and educational philosophers believe that engaging students in the creative arts is a step toward helping them find meaning in this complex world. Years ago, John Dewey recognized the value of art in shaking us loose from conventional, routine ways of seeing the world.[9] Howard Gardner argues that creating in the arts is a symbolic activity that inevitably creates meaning, because it requires the imagination to be engaged not only in problem *solving* but also in "equally creative problem *production*"[10] (italics mine). Creating art necessitates exploring the individual universe and allows the artist to express deeply significant ideas and emotions that are difficult both to understand and to express through "ordinary conversational language."[11]

Our capacity for taking in and processing information, says Jerome Bruner, is very limited, and so we must "compact vast ranges of experience in economical symbols — concepts, language, metaphor, myth, formulae. The price of failing at this art is either to be trapped in a confined world of experience or to be the victim of an overload of information."[12]

One important function of the creative arts is to facilitate the act of symbolizing, which Susanne Langer says human beings must do to make meaning of the world. I love her list of things that lie behind observable phenomena for each of us:

> Between the facts run the threads of unrecorded reality, momentarily recognized, wherever they come to the surface ... the bright, twisted threads of symbolic envisagement, imagination, thought-memory and reconstructed memory, belief beyond experience, dream, make-believe, hypotheses, philosophy—the whole creative process of ideation, metaphor, and abstraction that makes human life an adventure in understanding.[13]

Helping students simply be alert to the world around them has become an important job for teachers today, when the young spend large parts of their lives passively receiving information and images. Poetry writing encourages wide-awake observation of the world: To write about life, the poet must observe life. Often the very act of observing and recording in words leads to insight and a sense of meaning. Virginia Woolf speaks of the "shocks of awareness" that come to us occasionally, seeming to indicate some real thing behind an experience, and she says, "I make it real by putting it into words."[14]

So much of what we do in school asks students to learn passively, to take knowledge second-hand and simply commit it to memory, rather than asking them to learn through the exertions and focus of their own minds. Poetry writing can help form a connection between information in the world as objectively experienced and the subjectivity of the observer. Says Bruner: "Creative products have this power of reordering experience and thought in their image. In science, the reordering is much the same from one beholder of a formula to another. In art, the imitation is in part self-imitation ... the effective surprise of the creative [person] provides a new instrument for manipulating the world."[15]

Teachers who work with students on poetry writing see how much these forays into discovery affect students' thinking.

Tolerating Ambiguity

*Poetry is the art of understanding
what it is to be alive.*

—Archibald MacLeish

Our students are growing up in the computer and electronic age, the age of the quick fix. Advertising tells us every problem has a solution, often in consumerism. For anything really uncomfortable there's a drug: "Just take three of these." Armed with remote controls, we can switch continuously around the television dial; we can shop from our living room sofas. Fast-food restaurants and microwave ovens allow us instantly to gratify our desire to eat.

At the same time, this is an ambiguous world, probably even more ambiguous than it was a few decades ago. How can we help students tolerate—and even appreciate—ambiguity? Robert Sternberg points to tolerance of ambiguity as one of the essential attributes of the creative mind.[16] Reading and writing poetry both promote such a tolerance. The possibilities that works of art suggest, says Maxine Greene, are endless. "Unlike empirical problems and possibilities, they cannot be solved or resolved; there is always something more."[17] Many students find open-endedness unnerving, but after initial uneasiness with the lack of absolutes in an artistic enterprise such as writing poetry, they often discover that they enjoy a situation in which there are no unambiguously right and wrong answers, or even a single best approach.

The Search for Self

> In the very essence of poetry there is something
> indecent:
> A thing is brought forth that we didn't know we
> had in us,
> So we blink our eyes, as if a tiger had sprung out....
>
> —Czeslaw Milosz

At least as important as investing meaning in the world is the way writing poetry leads to self-discovery and to making sense of our own experiences, thoughts, and emotions. Because it is subjective, poetry encourages writers to tap into the unconscious mind in a way that transactional writing, with its emphasis on objectivity, does not. Poetry arouses an urgency to express the self, and the resulting writing is often far more profound than a prose exposition on an assigned topic. Poetry allows students to draw from a greater depth for sources of material. As James Britton says, "Poetry arises when something *needs to be said*, and the need is satisfied in the mere saying.... Poetry will tend to deal not with the trivial, conventionally social aspects of experience, but with what Coleridge referred to as 'the all in each of every man.'"[18] Maxine Greene speaks of the importance of helping our students discover themselves by first being attentive to the world and then filtering what they have noticed through their own conscious-ness, to come to a deeper knowledge of themselves. Turning experience into art requires both self-reflection and an awareness of one's own "life-world"; urging young people to create "is in part a process of liberating them for ... seeing beyond the actual and for pursuing themselves."[19]

The view of one tenth-grade student is revealed in an unsolicited notebook entry:

Just a personal opinion ...

I've been thinking a lot about poetry, and I've decided that it is one of the most fascinating ways to express a feeling or thought. Sometimes I even find out things about myself when I write. Actually, I almost always do, but poetry is exceptional that way. When I am able to really describe my feeling or thought in a poem, there is so much satisfaction, especially when the feeling can be "translated" by readers. Then there are the times that you write a poem for yourself, and you don't want others to understand. That's really special.

BUILDING SELF-ESTEEM

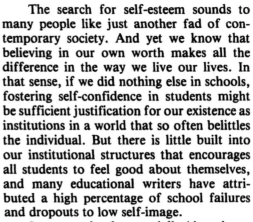

And if you include me among the lyric
poets, I'll hold my head so high it'll
strike the stars.

—Horace

The search for self-esteem sounds to many people like just another fad of contemporary society. And yet we know that believing in our own worth makes all the difference in the way we live our lives. In that sense, if we did nothing else in schools, fostering self-confidence in students might be sufficient justification for our existence as institutions in a world that so often belittles the individual. But there is little built into our institutional structures that encourages all students to feel good about themselves, and many educational writers have attributed a high percentage of school failures and dropouts to low self-image.

In many schools, especially (though not exclusively) large urban high schools, almost total anonymity is possible. Students can go through days without being noticed by anybody; they might as well not be there. So many voices go unheard! Perhaps all that is necessary to affirm those voices is to give them an opportunity to be heard and a response that shows someone is listening. Teachers also need to find ways in which we can reward students honestly for their efforts: "The really important task of teachers is conferring respect on those to whom respect is stingily given or denied altogether."[20]

Writing poetry gives all students a chance to express themselves in a way that cannot incur a judgment of right or wrong. In the writing workshop and in the poetry writing class, every voice can be heard, every expression and experience validated. As different learning styles are recognized and given an opportunity for expression, students who have not previously achieved in school may find that they understand course materials in a new way and become not only more successful but also more valued by teachers, other students, and themselves. These students can earn the respect they have so scantily received, increasing their self-respect and raising the odds of their being successful another time.

PRACTICAL CONSIDERATIONS:
TESTING AND COLLEGE PREPARATION

It makes you wonder, in the beginning
or the end (of the beginning),
if the skeletal design,
if globe and cosmos do not come down
to this ...

—Mark Rudman

Faced with the necessity of preparing students for state-mandated achievement tests, the Scholastic Aptitude Test, or Advanced Placement exams, you might say, "That's all very well, but what about the practical realities of life in schools? How can I take time for poetry when those tests loom so large? Students need to know how to choose the right answer and write analytical essays, not poetry. They can't even write decent job applications or college admissions essays, and you want me to waste time on poetry?"

But poetry writing helps students learn both effective self-expression and the basic language skills needed for tests; it is more effective than just memorizing lists of vocabulary or parts of speech, because it requires application. Struggling with the wording of poetry calls for precision and subtlety in vocabulary use and encourages sensitivity to language and grammatical construction. In *Frames of Mind*, Howard Gardner addresses this issue a number of times:

The poet must be superlatively sensitive to the shades of meanings of a word....

Whether it be the penning of a poem or the winning of a verbal joust, the precise choice of words proves important, if not all important....

In the poet ... one sees at work with special clarity the core operations of language. A sensitivity to the meaning of words, whereby an individual appreciates the subtle shades of difference between [words] ... a sensitivity to the order among words—the capacity to follow rules of grammar, and, on carefully selected occasions, to violate them. At a somewhat more sensory level—a sensitivity to the sounds, rhythms, inflections, and meters of words.... And a sensitivity to the different functions of language, its potential to excite, convince, stimulate, convey information, or simply to please.[21]

We could, I think, teach both vocabulary and grammar almost entirely through a series of lessons based on reading and writing poetry. Imagine, for example, a close reading of sections of Walt Whitman's *Song of Myself* that focuses on the poet's vocabulary, looking at not only the definitions of the words but the rich store of connotations as well. Consider alternative words—what test preparation books might call synonyms—and discuss the differences between them. Then ask students to put some of those words into an original poem, which requires a clear understanding of how the words are used. Or use a poem of Emily Dickinson's, look at her own alternative word choices, and discuss why she might have made her final decision. Have students take a poem of their own and consider changing words. Such activities necessitate using both a thesaurus to find synonyms and a dictionary to discover precise meanings and the connotations of words.

Understanding poetry also involves looking closely at the syntax and grammar of a poem. Ask your class to analyze syntax by finding the subject and verb of a poetic sentence, the antecedent of a pronoun, or the construction of a dependent clause. When it is appropriate, diagram a sentence on the chalkboard. Write some poems that follow set grammatical patterns, such as the diamanté, in which the seven lines must contain, in order: (1) one noun, (2) two adjectives, (3) three verbs or action participles, (4) a four-word phrase, (5) three verbs or participles, (6) two adjectives, and (7) one noun.

Revision exercises offer another way to strengthen language skills. When students revise their own poetry, they must understand the grammatical concepts involved as they scrutinize their use of nouns or verbs, question the use of adverbs, examine the clarity of dependent clauses, and so on. Checking an original poem for unintentional word repetition, redundancy, and precision in wording makes students sensitive to nuances in language.

Poetry reading and writing encourage close reading for detail and making inferences, both reading skills that are tested on standardized tests. As for the English Advanced Placement test, poetry writing teaches careful poetry reading, and to struggle with their own words and images in a formal literary way leads students to understand other poets' choices: Being analytical about their own writing sharpens their critical faculty in analyzing literature. The relationship between poetry writing and facility with expository prose will help students write better on tests such as the English Composition achievement test, which require quick and natural essays of personal response.

College application essays seem difficult, I think, in part because we have so often made students be objective and analytical in their writing, omitting the personal. When they are asked suddenly to write about themselves in an interesting way, they cannot make the switch from impersonal formality to fluent subjectivity. Poetry writing can only help in this process of expressing the self.

POETRY WRITING ACROSS THE CURRICULUM

As poet and mathematician, he would reason well; as mere mathematician, he would not have reasoned at all.

—Edgar Allan Poe

Poetry is the breath and finer spirit of all knowledge; it is the impassioned expression which is the countenance of all science.

—William Wordsworth

"Writing across the curriculum" has been widely urged by experts in the writing field, who have shown over and over the learning value of writing in every academic discipline and of writing in more than the transactional or expository mode. Teachers of many subjects who have experimented with expressive writing, including student journals and personal reflections on learning and problem-solving methods, have found such writing to be a powerful learning tool.

If the preceding arguments for poetry are valid for the English class, they apply to other subject areas as well. Discovery, divergent thinking, creativity, intuition, metaphorical thinking, tolerance of ambiguity, and self-esteem are important for students in any discipline. Poetry writing taps into the imagination, the unconscious, and underlying knowledge structures. It encourages imaginative leaps in thinking. It helps students make new connections, look at course material from different perspectives, think in new ways, make material meaningful by discovering personal relations to it, and be surprised by new insights. For many students, a poetic response brings content to life and makes it memorable. Teachers support different learning styles when we encourage writing all along the continuum that reaches from the transactional to the poetic.

Thinking processes apparently differ surprisingly little from discipline to discipline. "Reasoning by analogy and communicating by metaphor are generally recognized as strategies of successful thinkers and writers in every discipline," says Art Young.[22] Both Howard Gardner and Jerome Bruner stress the value of metaphorical thinking for discovery and learning in all intellectual endeavors, not just in art. "Experience in literal terms is a categorizing, a placing in a syntax of concept. Metaphoric combination leaps beyond systematic placement, explores connections that before were unsuspected."[23] Gardner calls the ability to see resemblances between disparate things a high act of creativity in all kinds of thinking, and he points to the frequency with which scientific breakthroughs are described in metaphorical terms.[24] He suggests that children should be taught in a systematic way to create metaphor.

Robert Frost maintained that all thinking, except mathematical thinking, is metaphorical, but I believe he stopped too soon by not including mathematical thinking. Jacques Maritain said that "there is poetry involved in the work of all great mathematicians" and philosophers and that "poetry ... extends ... beyond the realm of art.... A kind of poetic intuition can come into play everywhere—in science, philosophy, big business, revolution, religion ... when the mind of man attains to a certain depth of mastery in the power of discovering new horizons and taking great risks."[25]

Teachers in all subject areas can use poetry writing assignments to achieve a variety of pedagogical aims. For some students, the freer structures of poetry clarify and increase understanding of a concept. Working with course materials in a different way may help students see whether the material has actually been learned. When the format for handling content is always question-and-answer or linear exposition, it is possible for both student and teacher to believe that material has been learned because the student has done well on a test of facts. Trying to use the material in new situations and with new applications may reveal a lack of real grasp of concepts. When students write a poem about some aspect of the material, they may understand and internalize it in a different way. Writing poetry can also make course content more memorable; doing something out of the ordinary often has this effect.

Joan Guest, a science teacher in my school, asks her eighth-grade science students to write a poem about a light beam's journey from the sun to the Earth through various obstacles the beam encounters. The assignment makes students clarify the concepts they have learned by using the material in a different intellectual construct. I asked Guest's students to evaluate the assignment for me. Their comments included:

I enjoyed this assignment very much because I was able to apply what I had learned to a different [form than] a test.

It made me think in a different way. Text book material is fine for automatons, but we are humans and humans enjoy using their imaginations.

I don't usually like doing this kind of assignment. But I found it kind of fun and a good way to organize my knowledge on light. The only thing was I wasn't sure how much detail to add.

It was fun to find words that rhyme. The poem also helped me to study and understand light in that way.

I always like writing poems, sayings, and different key clues to help me remember something. I wrote my poem in the colors of the rainbow to help me remember the order of the colors.

I usually forget things after the test is over, but by having funny ways to think of and remember things, I remember them longer.

In a Canadian school, a chemistry teacher asked fourteen- and fifteen-year-old students to write a poem about ammonia chemistry. The teacher saw the writing of a poem as "the culmination of a complex, internalised process" that, "like problem solving ... is a multistage process involving creative thinking."[26]

Playful poetry writing may help some students loosen up and feel comfortable with the terms and vocabulary of a discipline as well as its concepts. It may also help students feel that the disciplines are not quite as separated as school structures often suggest. Some surprising metaphors can emerge. One student's science/math love poem included the lines

> I want you to hug me like a focus
> wants to be hugged by a parabola.
> You are the flint that lights
> my Bunsen burner.
>
> —Aparna Chowdhury, Grade 10

Poetry may make course content significant by personalizing it. For example, in a history class preparing to do a role play on some historical moment or issue, a persona poem, in which the students write in the voice of the character they are going to play, can make that character come alive to them. Before a debate, writing a poem on the topic provides a second, subjective perspective on material that has been logically organized, and it also may raise new insights, lending conviction to the subsequent presentation.

Poetry writing can be used to summarize course material and to review it. Art Young describes a college philosophy class in which the teacher, with strong reservations, assigned a poem as a final review of Descartes's "Meditations."[27]

Some of the students' responses to the assignment in a subsequent evaluation said:

It forces the student to think about what he is doing, and in the process sets off a chain reaction of thinking about the subject and things related to the subject.

Most of the time I surprised myself along the way. It is interesting to see how my mind develops an idea to a point I haven't planned.

I enjoyed writing the poem, just to know I could write one and be a little creative.

I have the freedom to change anything. I can write anything I want and know that there is no wrong answer.

It made me go over the reading more carefully than I had done before ... this experience resulted in a more thorough understanding and a deeper learning.

It was fun and at the same time it was a good review. It gave me a chance to pick out key points and stress them. I am sure they will stay with me longer.

The professor commented: "I am convinced that the majority of my students reread the 'Meditations' and seriously tried to understand what Descartes is saying. I regard this assignment [on which he had embarked with 'considerable trepidation'] as a definite pedagogical success. The assignment produced ... surprises for me ... the unexpected high number of 'good' poems ... the enthusiasm of many of the students."

The professor's remaining reservation was "the propriety of giving students homework which has virtually no impact on their grade." But from the students' evaluations and his own admission, most of them worked hard on the assignment, took it seriously, enjoyed it, learned from it, and felt freed from the constraints of being graded or judged right or wrong. As long as we pessimistically believe that students will never work or learn without the "stick" of a grade to impel them, we will never be released from the tyranny of the almighty gradebook.

NOTES

[1]Maxine Greene. "Breaking Through the Ordinary: The Arts and Future Possibility." *Journal of Education*, vol. 162, no. 3, 1980, 20.

[2]Howard Gardner. *Frames of Mind*. New York: Basic Books, 1983.

[3]Kenneth E. Eble. "Educating Ritas: A Different Kind of Competence." *Educational Horizons*, spec. issue, 1985.

[4]Peter Elbow. *Embracing Contraries*. New York and Oxford: Oxford University Press, 1986, 62.

[5]Greene, "Breaking Through the Ordinary," 20.

[6]James Britton. *Language and Learning*. Middlesex, England: Penguin Books, 1970.

[7]Jacques Maritain. *Creative Intuition in Art and Poetry*. Cleveland and New York: Meridian Books, 1953, 99. The quotations that follow are included in Maritain, 247.

[8]Elbow, 55-62.

[9]John Dewey. *Art as Experience*. New York: Putnam, 1954.

[10]Howard Gardner. *Art, Mind, and Brain*. New York: Basic Books, 1982, 44.

[11]Ibid., 90.

[12]Jerome Bruner. *On Knowing*. Cambridge, MA, and London: Belknap Press of Harvard University Press, 1982, 7.

[13]Susanne K. Langer. *Philosophy in a New Key*. Cambridge, MA, and London: Harvard University Press, 1942, 281.

[14]Virginia Woolf. "A Sketch of the Past," in *Moments of Being: Unpublished Autobiographical Writings*, ed. Jeanne Schulkind. New York: Harcourt Brace Jovanovich, 1976, 70.

[15]Bruner, 22.

[16]Robert J. Sternberg. Lecture delivered at Teachers College, Columbia University, 1989.

[17]Maxine Greene. *Landscapes of Learning*. New York and London: Teachers College Press, 1978, 202.

[18]Britton, 120.

[19]Greene, *Landscapes of Learning*, 182.

[20]Eble, 46.

[21]Gardner, *Frames of Mind*, 75-83.

[22]Art Young. "Considering Values: The Poetic Function of Language," in Toby Fulweiler and Art Young, *Language Connections*. Urbana, IL: NCTE, 1982, 78.

[23]Bruner, 20.

[24]Gardner, *Frames of Mind*, 96.

[25]Maritain, 237.

[26]D. J. Jones. *Chem 13 News*, April 1989.

[27]Young, 88-91.

Oh! Many are the poets that are sown
By Nature; men [sic] endowed with highest gifts,
The vision and the faculty divine;
Yet wanting the accomplishment of verse.

—William Wordsworth

Most educators agree that critical thinking is an important skill to teach, and materials for working on that skill have become quite plentiful. Perhaps because our society emphasizes the logical-rational mode of thinking, or because we assume that the imaginative realm of a person's mind will develop without special attention, teaching creative thinking has not yet received the same degree of support, although new trends seem to be moving in that direction. Howard Gardner stresses the importance of cultivating imaginative thinking: "The advent and maturing of literary imagination is not a foregone conclusion. Just as a child's logical understanding of the world must be constructed, so must his [sic] ability to engage in pretense and fantasy."[1]

Helping young people create poetry is one excellent way to expand and encourage the imagination. But it is not enough simply to ask them to write: The teacher must spark their creativity and then help them learn how to write well, to formulate their poetic statements with care, not just spill out raw emotions or experience. Meaning and self-discovery come as much through shaping and articulating experience as through recognizing it. We can help students find and express their vision and understanding, expand their search for meaning, increase their skill and pleasure in using language, and grow in self-confidence as they take pride in the precision and quality of their writing. Writing poetry, discussing it, and revising and polishing it encourage creative and critical thinking to work together in the most positive way.

The next several chapters offer suggestions for planning and carrying out a program of poetry writing that may be included systematically in a class throughout the school year. The program described in this chapter is appropriate for both middle and high school students. The class method has its roots in the writing workshop model, with emphasis on the writing process, revision, and collaborative learning through peer review.

ELEMENTS OF THE PROGRAM

Writing Groups

An appreciative audience for writing is always important, especially for poetry, which is both very personal and a great equalizer of student writers. In the poetry class, every voice can be heard and responded to positively. For this purpose, it is essential to divide the class into the smaller units of writing groups.

17

The size of groups will depend on the size of your class; I find groups of four or five most comfortable.

Writing groups that function well provide the best kind of collaborative learning: Students work together with a real learning task that is important to them. The group's work is to help each member become a better writer, by reading and commenting on each other's writing. Groups offer support and encouragement as well as specific suggestions for ways to improve a poem. After the group has read a number of works by the same writer, they will begin to pick up general strengths and problems to discuss as well as those peculiar to a single poem. Each member of the group is responsible for responding to every piece of writing and should be held to that task: One of the best ways to recognize and solve the problems of your own writing is to see the problems in other people's.

Sharing poetry in writing groups is easiest when the writer can pass out copies of the poem to each member and then read it aloud. If giving copies is not possible, the writer should read the poem aloud slowly and clearly, showing it to the group as necessary. Either way, a poem ideally should be read twice before it is discussed.

Students need to learn how to comment constructively. One tendency is to say simply, "Oh, that's good!"—although ego gratifying, just about the least helpful comment a writer can get. (The only one worse is a blanket condemnation.) Responses should always begin with the positive, as group members in turn tell the writer what they particularly like about the poem. Then they can move to questions about parts that need clarification, about the source of the poem to elicit more detail, or about the writer's choice of specific words, figures, images, and so on. Mary Strong and Mimi Neamen call this procedure the "P's and Q's" of response: Praise first, then Question.[2]

Good ways for writing groups to respond include the following:

- Point out the strengths of a poem, either as an overall comment or, more usefully, regarding specific places that affected the reader. Try to analyze, as a group, why certain elements are effective.

- Ask questions for clarification.

- Ask questions for expansion.

- Ask for rereading of a particular part of a poem for comment or questions.

- Ask the writer questions about the source of the poem, its impulse or vision; suggest looking again at the origin to see whether the poem has captured the vision.

- Ask why. For example, question the writer's specific choices in narrative voice, words, imagery, stanza order, form, verb tense, or punctuation.

- Ask the writer to show instead of tell.

- Ask whether everything in the poem is necessary.

- Consider any or all of the technical elements of poetry writing discussed in chapter 5.

- Focus on shared problems raised by a particular assignment.

- Make suggestions for revision, not by actually doing the rewriting but by pointing out places to consider revising.

The author of a piece is responsible for not letting the group finish with its review after a few superficial comments and should push them to go more deeply into the poem. The writer may ask questions or offer alternatives for the group to consider. Minimize defensive reactions: Make it clear to the groups that even the very best works still have room for improvement. Students should also understand that the author always has the last word and need not do everything a group suggests.

After the group has finished discussing each poem, and the writers are all satisfied with the length and quality of the responses, they should turn to quiet revising until all groups are done. Don't let students just sit and chat; that not only distracts other groups but also suggests that the work of the group is not serious.

If writing groups are to work well during the year, they need plenty of support at the beginning. Students who have never participated in writing groups before must learn how to function effectively. I usually spend time on building supportive groups to make students very aware of the collaborative process and the power of collaboration. This can be done through narratives: My first writing assignment before introducing poetry is to ask students to describe a time they were a member of a group. They tell whether the group functioned very well or very badly and then analyze what made the group succeed or fail and what they did or might have done to create a strong group. As members read the narratives to each other in writing groups, they discuss the group process and how they can make their particular group successful.

Sometimes it helps to model group responses by bringing in students from a previous class. If your class is small, you might try doing the first few sessions with the whole class working together as a writing group, to experiment with responses to writing. Or have one group volunteer to serve as "guinea pigs" for the rest of the class to observe; then ask the class to analyze their use of the group process.

As groups become more and more proficient at responding, they may find themselves deciding that they will all try a particular type of poem or will all write on the same topic; sometimes they may want to work on a collaborative poem. Good collaborative groups will have a very strong effect on each other's writing and understanding of poetry. Periodically, students should be asked, both as a group and individually, to critique the group process and make suggestions for improving it.

Writing Process

In all kinds of writing, including poetry, students should be made aware of the writing process, from the first generative prewriting stages, through drafts, revision, and editing, to the final copy.

Prewriting. Prewriting in the poetry program may take a number of forms: reading and discussing poetry in class, notebook entries (see chapter 3, "The

Writer's Notebook"), and various exercises to bring material from the mind to paper in crude form. Freewriting is one of the best exercises to generate writing material. The writer must keep pen or pencil moving steadily for a timed period, usually five to ten minutes, writing quickly in a stream of consciousness without interposing any editorial judgment and without paying attention to spelling, punctuation, or grammar. The only rule is to keep writing, even if what you write is only "My hand hurts" or "I don't have anything to say." The aim is to tap the resources of the mind for writing material; unexpected ideas, memories, details, or images often emerge when the writer does not pause to shape or correct what is being written. Freewriting may be completely open to any idea that comes along or it may focus on a single incident or topic.

Students are usually able to bring out quantities of useful detail by "looping." After they do a freewriting, ask them to read through what they have written and circle one word or phrase they would like to write more about. Then have them do a second freewriting starting from that word. Circling again and doing yet a third freewriting begins to shape and define the focus of a piece of writing.

In *Writing the Natural Way*, Gabriele Lusser Rico describes another way of opening up the mind: clustering.[3] With clustering, the writer collects associations around a key word or short phrase, the intended topic for writing. Write the word or phrase in the center of a piece of paper and circle it; then write down and circle every word or phrase that comes to mind, connecting the circles with lines that emanate from the central idea (fig. 2.1). Let ideas spring from each other to form chains of association; go back to the center to begin another chain whenever a new idea occurs. Figure 2.1 is a cluster I formed in about three minutes around the key word *time*.

Fig. 2.1. Clustering.

Revision. Revision is at least as important for poetry as for any other kind of writing—perhaps more important. At the same time, it is somewhat more delicate to suggest revision in poetry than in expository writing, because students often are more personally invested in what they have written. Many young poets initially do not believe they need to revise; they think poetry should "just come." Thinking of the etymology of the word *revise*—to "look at again," to "re-see"—will help them understand "re-vision" as meaning more than just correcting spelling or adding or deleting a few words. It suggests looking again, not just at the words but also at the original vision from which the poem arose. After this examination the writer may want to clarify the vision, restructure it, change its direction or focus, add details, or delete unnecessary parts.

Often, leaving a poem alone for several days and then coming back to it will make the need for revision clearer; immediately after writing, authors see what they *think* they have written, rather than what they really have written. I urge my students to let all their writing "age" so they can come back to it with fresh eyes. I don't expect students to have a final copy of a poem on the date the assignment is due, but I do expect a serious draft. Revision is an ongoing process, and finished work should be turned in by periodic deadlines. Specific suggestions for helping students revise are included in chapter 5, "Teaching Poetry Writing."

Editing and Proofreading. Editing, which takes place after the last revision, entails the preparation of what writers of the nineteenth century called a "fair copy," a copy of the poem in its final form, ready for publication. At this stage, students should check spelling and punctuation carefully and look at the grammar once again. After the finished copy is written or printed out, it should be proofread for inadvertent copying or typographical errors.

Editing and proofreading make most sense to students when they have a reason for making their best effort. The teacher may give deadlines for completing a portfolio, or collection of finished poems, two or three times in a marking period. Deadlines are most natural when you can link them to actual dates for publication of the students' poetry in some form.

The Writer's Notebook

The writer's notebook, which differs somewhat from a standard journal, is an important element of the poetry writing program. It is described in detail in chapter 3.

Folders

Students should always keep all their work together in file folders so it is available for a variety of uses in the writing workshop. Using separate folders for works-in-progress and finished poems helps student writers keep track of their efforts, and they can take satisfaction in seeing the finished work accumulate. I like students to have another separate folder in which they can store rejected bits: Discarding pieces is easier if you know they are not gone forever. An abandoned poem may well be picked up later when the time is right and reworked; often a stanza, line, phrase, or image can be recycled into another piece of work.

Using Computers

If your school has computers that are available to the students, be sure to use this opportunity for teaching your class to use the word processor in their writing. Most students really enjoy working with the computer once they feel comfortable with its basic use, but they must be taught how to use it to strengthen, not just to simplify, writing.

Some students are inclined to write quickly at the computer and simply print out the result, turning it in as finished work. But the real advantage of the word processor is that it makes revision much easier, both for radical change (cutting, moving text, or inserting) and for fine-tuning sentences, words, and punctuation. It is hard, though, to see what needs revising just by looking at the screen. Teach students the value of printing out drafts and show them how to work back and forth from their printouts to the computer. Help them determine the writing process that works best for them: Some people write their best drafts right on the computer; others prefer to write the first draft by hand and then type it into the computer before starting revision. In either case, emphasize the importance of constantly saving work and printing it out for the revision process.

The word processor offers almost unlimited opportunities for playing and experimenting with poetry. You have an ideal situation if you can take a whole class into the computer room during occasional poetry writing periods and use that time as an experimental session. Give a specific revision assignment, such as varying line lengths and changing line breaks—tedious to do by hand but easy on the word processor. Ask students to experiment with mixing up the order of stanzas in a poem. Have them print out the various versions, and then devote some time in writing groups to discussing the results. In all the poetry experimentation, make sure students print out each draft of their poems and label the draft to show its place in the sequence of revisions before they put it in their folders. Often they will want to reverse changes and go back to parts, at least, of earlier drafts.

Some software programs for poetry writing exist. Although such programs deal primarily with rather mechanical forms of poetry, they may help interest some of your students in writing poems, especially the very technologically minded. I might use the programs occasionally to stimulate writing but certainly not as the major way to approach poetry writing.

Publication

Students need a variety of audiences to read as well as to hear their poetry; their work should be aired as often as you can create an opportunity for them to share it with their class, the school, parents, other schools, and the public. The following lists suggest ways of developing an audience for student poetry.

Share Poetry in Your Classroom

- A constantly renewed bulletin board of poems is the very simplest way to provide an audience.

- Be sure that all classmates hear each other's poetry. Occasionally have groups choose one poem to read to the whole class. Set aside a class period now and then for a poetry reading period in which you give every student a certain amount of time to read.

- Periodically, make a class collection of finished works or bits from favorite notebook entries. Photocopying a class publication doesn't take much of your time if you give each student one or two sheets of paper on which to write out whatever they want to include. If they like, students may illustrate their pages, or they may give them to a classmate to illustrate. Make a copy of the whole collection for each student.

- Make students' portfolios of finished poetry available for classmates to read.

Enlarge the Audience for Poetry in Your School

- Give the library a few copies of class publications. Find ways to work with your librarian to create a space for school and class publications in the library.

- Share class publications with other teachers and administrators.

- Start a constantly changing schoolwide bulletin board for poetry.

- Find another teacher who is interested in poetry writing and form a collaboration between classes to share students' work.

- Establish a poetry computer link with another class.

- Form a one-on-one buddy system with students from another class to read and comment on each other's poetry.

- Have students read their poems to slightly younger classes.

- Start a "round-robin" circulating poetry collection among classes in the school (each class contributes poems and, as the collection circulates, reads other classes' contributions, removes their own previous poems, and adds new ones).

- Work closely with the school literary magazine, and make sure your students submit poems. If your school doesn't have a literary magazine, investigate ways to start one. The magazine doesn't need to be terribly fancy, only to provide a reading public for student writing.

- Run poetry contests within the school but don't make poetry a win/lose activity by awarding first, second, and third prizes. Make sure that all students who enter are recognized and rewarded for their efforts. Arrange a poetry reading or a special publication of contest poems. Give a celebration party (with good refreshments and a reading) for contestants. Single out each entrant for special praise; have judges who are not the student's teacher comment, privately or publicly, on the best feature of each poem. Recognize participants' efforts at an awards assembly.

- Help students from your class or the literary magazine staff organize and run poetry workshops for other students during an assembly or club period to encourage poetry writing in the school.

- Lobby for a poetry day or poetry assembly in the school. Try to make student poetry a frequent feature of assemblies and other gatherings; encourage poems written for special occasions, such as a class poem for graduation.

- Sponsor a "coffee house" poetry reading time, at lunch or during an assembly period.

- Get poetry included at least once a week in daily announcements.

- Help students start a creative writing club.

- Start a series of "class poems" beginning with a provocative line from a poem; each writer adds a line and folds the sheet over, leaving only the last line as a springboard for the next writer.

Involve Parents as an Audience

- Make sure parents see copies of class publications by sending publications home and by displaying them at back-to-school evenings, parent-teacher conferences, and so on.

- Sponsor a "coffee house" or poetry reading evening for students and parents. Encourage parents to participate in the readings as well.

- If your school puts on a talent show or cabaret evening, be sure poetry reading is part of it.

- Work with teachers in the art, music, and drama departments to put on an arts festival that includes poetry.

Share Poetry Writing with Other Schools

- Join with a class in another school to share poetry, through either the mail or (even more fun) a computer link.

- Find a class in another school with whom individual students may become "poetry pals" for reading and comment.

- Share literary magazines with other schools. This is particularly useful when the students can meet each other or otherwise communicate personally about the work.

- Sponsor a poetry reading exchange with other local schools.

- Sponsor a poetry club with members from different schools.

- Sponsor a poetry festival with other local schools.

Provide Students with a Wider Public Audience

- Try to include student poetry in school publications such as school district newsletters or alumni magazines.

- Encourage students to submit poetry to local or regional teen arts festivals.

- Seek out local and national writing contests, such as the Scholastic writing competition or Princeton University's poetry contest for high school juniors, and help your students submit work. (English department chairs receive notice of many contests each year. Make sure the information gets shared.)

- Encourage (and help) students to submit work to local and national magazines such as *Merlyn's Pen*, *Stone Soup*, *Scholastic*, Susquehanna University's *Apprentice Writer*, and others. One of your deadlines might be a required submission of work to a contest or publication.

Consider encouraging the faculty in your school to write by starting a teachers' writing group and urging them to publish poems in the literary magazine, read at your "coffee house," and in other ways show students that poetry is a serious adult enterprise.

Reading Poetry

The best way for students to love poetry and want to write is to read widely in poetry. The sounds of good poetry provide a powerful example of poetic expression; imagery triggers the imagination; the voices heard in reading poetry inspire writers to raise their own voices.

Read poetry with your students often, rather than just once a year in a special unit. Poems don't always have to be formally analyzed and explicated. Frequent reading, with students and teacher pointing out details they like, asking questions, and discussing poems without necessarily reaching a conclusion, will teach students to enjoy poetry and to pay attention to the details of how it works. Choose good poetry, truthful poetry, poetry you like. The poems should be accessible to students, but don't underestimate their taste and capacities. Kenneth Koch has demonstrated that even the youngest children can enjoy the best poetry.[4] Students like both narrative and lyric poetry. Look for poems that contain vivid images, arresting words and sounds, and an interesting, authentic voice, poems that pique the curiosity and present the world in a new way.

Poetry is meant to be heard. The class should hear it read aloud often and should become used to listening to the works of the best poets—and to their own as well. Students need to learn how to read poetry aloud; give them frequent practice in oral interpretation, as well as letting them hear you model poetry reading. Choral reading is an enjoyable way to give students a feeling for both rhythm and tone in poetry. Video and cassette tapes of poets reading their own work help students hear the relationship between the spoken and written word.

THE TEACHER'S ROLE

The teacher of poetry writing has a major and active role to play in the program. As poetry writing coach, the teacher stimulates, encourages, and helps student writers develop skill and technique in their imaginative forays. A number of exercises and class activities aimed at these goals are detailed in chapter 4, "Getting Started," and chapter 5, "Teaching Poetry Writing."

Beginning poetry writers also need suggestions for topics. "Write a poem" is not an adequate assignment; students must be given an idea as a springboard from which to start if they are not to write trite and predictable poems. Of course, poetry writers can always deviate from the original idea or assignment and go off on their own tack. Suggestions for developing poetry assignments are given in chapters 6 and 7.

I usually give students a chance to begin their writing in class after a prewriting activity and talking about the assignment. Often the spontaneous response to a stimulating assignment will get a poem going better than if students began laboriously, after long thought, at home. While they are writing, you can circulate and look at what students are doing, encouraging their writing by praising a felicitous line or word, by asking questions, or by answering questions.

Try to meet frequently with individual students to talk about their poetry in writing conferences. When groups have finished discussion and are working on revision, you can often find time for a few quick conferences; occasionally you might meet with a few students during the writing group time. Conferences may be as brief as a minute or two, or longer if the student wants to go over several poems or has many questions. The most helpful kind of conference is one in which the teacher asks questions to help the student clarify, re-see the poem, take risks, or stretch verbally. By talking about their poems, you can lead students to be more imaginative, specific, and precise. Although conferences should be encouraging rather than judgmental, evaluation is an important part of the meeting.

Another important role for the poetry teacher is to model the writing process by writing along with students: to be a *writing teacher* in both senses of the phrase. Let students see you working out the issues poetry writing raises: Share not only your finished work, but also your struggle with the problems students themselves are working through. Do this not as the expert who has the answers but as a fellow seeker and learner. Help students understand the ongoing nature of learning to write, and show by example that the process of working toward precision in self-expression is part of the pleasure as well as the challenge of writing. Watching their teacher seek solutions for the same difficulties and complexities they are dealing with—and find joy in the process—encourages and supports students. It is also partly a matter of honesty: Why should they believe poetry writing is important if they don't see that it is important for us?

Some ways to share the process with your students follow:

- Do each assignment with a class so you understand the particular problems the assignment raises. Talk freely about the topic and how you approached it, while encouraging students to discuss their own ways of solving the difficulties. Make the process of writing an important part of the discussions.

- Use a poem you recently wrote as an idea for a writing topic. Tell students what triggered the poem or how you arrived at the idea. Ask for volunteers among students who write unassigned poetry to do the same thing with one of their poems.

- Use an unfinished poem-in-process as a model for group discussion. Help students see what questions to ask each other about their poems and what elements of poetry to examine in the writing groups.

- Join a writing group sometimes, as just another member with similar problems, questions, and suggestions.

- Put a draft of one of your poems on the overhead projector and have students help you do some revisions. Point out problems you're having and parts you're not satisfied with; ask for their help.

- Put one of your poems on a computer disk and encourage students to play around with changing stanza order, line length, and other aspects.

- Let students see the finished version of a poem they have seen in draft. Discuss what you accepted from their comments and what you didn't, and offer the reasons for your decisions.

- Show students a finished poem along with all the drafts you did before the final version. Talk about the process of revision and why you made the changes you did. Discuss the vision and re-vision of the poem.

- Start writing a poem on the board and talk about what you're doing. Make it a joint teacher-student poem.

- Be sure to join in on all publications — bulletin board, class collections, literary magazine, etc. — and poetry readings.

When students and teacher learn together, wonderful things can happen with poetry — both for them and for you. In fact, I started seriously writing poetry myself only when I was doing it along with my students.

EVALUATING STUDENTS' POETRY

Grading poetry is, I find, a touchy and rather explosive issue among teachers. Almost all professional poet/teachers insist that students' poetry should not be graded (read Kenneth Koch,[5] Alan Ziegler,[6] and Jack Collom,[7] for example). Anyone who writes poetry and has had it commented on can attest to the wide disparity of reactions to a poem even from people who are deeply involved in poetry professionally. One poem I wrote in a writing workshop moved my teacher to say, "I feel vindicated as a teacher; this is really powerful," while a friend, also a poet and teacher, said of the same poem, "This is a pack of scattered shards."

I believe students' poetry should not be given letter grades. Even though we know that grading of all writing is somewhat subjective, in most expository assignments grading is done according to specific guidelines. In poetry, the writer sets the standards for each poem. How can we stamp poems honestly with a comparative, competitive letter grade?

This is not, however, to say that we should not evaluate students' poetry. On the contrary, evaluation is an essential, ongoing feature of the poetry writing program. The teacher must be not only very responsive to what students write, but critical as well. Without evaluation, we encourage unthinking and uncritical writing from students. Taking students' poetry seriously enough to evaluate it carefully both dignifies their efforts and underlines the fact that you consider poetry writing an important part of your coursework.

Standards for good poetry writing are similar to those for any good writing, raised, perhaps, to the highest level. The first thing to notice about a poem, and call attention to, is whatever seems imaginative, creative, or insightful and gives delight. On a more formal level, control — of language (diction, syntax, and grammar), of voice, and of form — is the hallmark of a well-written poem. Helen Vendler has described how a good poem "enacts" its meaning through its formal elements: A bad poem merely says what it thinks, whereas a good one "finds a formal equivalency between statement and presentation."[8] In evaluating students' writing, look for a correspondence between topic and style: See whether a governing "law of the whole" exists in which strategies of presentation support the thought. Try to find the structure or shape of the whole first; then look at the decorative details. Consider all the questions that a writing group does, and always remember to mind the "P's and Q's" yourself: Begin with plenty of Praise before you start to Question.

One job of the teacher as responder is to help students learn to analyze, evaluate, and be critical of their own work. After all, the writers themselves are ultimately responsible for the quality of their work. The metaphor of writing teacher as coach and not umpire suits the purposes of poetry writing. Our goal is to hone skills, teach techniques, and help all students achieve their personal best: We should adopt the coach's methods and encourage progress, praising the good, pointing out techniques for improvement, and promoting the attitude that every new effort can be better than the last. The ends we seek are improved writing skills, self-expression, and learning—not to be a professional poet at age fifteen.

In that spirit, not all your comments need be positive. In fact, very specific suggestions for revision are called for. But comments should respond to what the student has actually set up in a poem and how well that aim has been achieved. A poem should never receive a negative response because the writer has not adhered to a specific assignment or particular way of writing. The teacher should know each student and gear comments to the individual, to raise all students above their current level of writing. Not everything a student writes needs a detailed response. Students should have the option every now and then of choosing not to have their poetry commented on, and teachers should have the option occasionally not to comment in depth.

Although the best forum for responding to poetry writing is a conference with a student, such a meeting is not always possible. Because written comments by a teacher always carry a particular weight of authority, they should be as supportive and nonthreatening as possible. At the same time, it is essential to point out weak areas and help students learn to identify such weaknesses for themselves. First focus on the strengths of the poem and then give helpful suggestions for revision. That doesn't mean actually making changes for students or giving them new wording or a different organizational pattern, but rather suggesting that they reconsider certain aspects of the poem, expand or condense some parts, reword or reorganize, and so on.

The teacher needs to be careful, especially in written comments, not to inhibit the writer or seem to be critical of the person. Some kinds of comments are thoroughly unhelpful because they are too general to give the writer a direction to move or because they simply arouse a defensive reaction. For example, the words *trite* and *cliché* are a slap to a student writer; the need for a fresh look can be suggested more gently ("I have heard that phrase—or metaphor, etc.—used before; is there a way you could find to say the same thing in new words?"). "This is not poetry" leads to the defensive response, "Who says?" Comments on the poem's subject, such as, "This topic is not interesting," "This is not deep enough," or "This doesn't say anything," are both insulting and unhelpful. Where do students go with that comment if the topic is important, interesting, or significant to them? And who determines the appropriate content for poetry?

Students should understand that the teacher's responses are the personal reactions of an experienced reader, expressing what you like about what they have written or what changes you think might improve a poem, and not absolute judgments—on either the poetry or them.

I like to have students periodically prepare a portfolio of finished poetry. A booklet with a table of contents (and illustrations, if they like) gives them—and me—a very satisfying sense of having produced a significant body of work. Portfolios should be shared through oral readings and should be available for perusal by classmates.

Contrary to the fear that ungraded work is taken less seriously by students than work that will be given a grade, I have found that students are more likely to have poetry assignments done on time and done carefully, to participate eagerly in writing groups, and to rewrite and revise. The motivation for poetry writing seems to have become internal rather than external; the students do care about expressing themselves in the most effective way. I base grades for poetry writing only on the fulfillment of requirements: doing assignments, participating in writing groups, and handing in finished work by the deadline.

Never tell a young poet all his faults.

—Ben Jonson

NOTES

[1]Howard Gardner. *Art, Mind, and Brain.* New York: Basic Books, 1982, 182.

[2]Mary Strong and Mimi Neamen. *Writing Through Children's Literature, Grades 3-8.* Englewood, CO: Teacher Ideas Press, forthcoming, 1993.

[3]Gabriele Lusser Rico. *Writing the Natural Way.* Los Angeles: J. P. Tarcher, 1983, 28-49.

[4]Kenneth Koch. *Rose, Where Did You Get That Red?"* New York: Vintage Books, 1974, 3-29.

[5]Ibid., 24.

[6]Alan Ziegler. *The Writing Workshop, Vol. 1.* New York: Teachers and Writers Collaborative, 1981, 24-26.

[7]Jack Collom. *Moving Windows: Evaluating the Poetry Children Write.* New York: Teachers and Writers Collaborative, 1985, 166.

[8]Helen Vendler. Seminar at Harvard University, 1989.

So the point of my keeping a notebook has never been ... to have an accurate factual record of what I have been doing or thinking.... Perhaps it never did snow that August in Vermont; perhaps there never were flurries in the night wind, and maybe no one else felt the ground hardening and summer already dead even as we pretended to bask in it, but that was how it felt to me, and it might as well have snowed, could have snowed, did snow. How it felt to me: that is getting closer to the truth about a notebook.

—Joan Didion

Try to be one of the people on whom nothing is lost.

—Henry James

Today most classes that deal with writing and the writing process include journal writing. The journal is used to generate ideas for writing, to accustom students to writing in the personal voice, and to give them a forum for expressing their feelings. I ask my students to emulate professional writers by keeping a writer's notebook as a resource for their writing.

The writer's notebook includes the aims of a journal but differs from it in significant ways. Emphasis shifts away from "dear diary" or "what I did today" entries to entries more specifically aimed at subsequent writing. The notebook becomes, like the professional writer's notebook, a storehouse not only of ideas, feelings, and experience but also of imaginative re-creations of experience, images, words, and phrases from which to draw in writing. It encourages students to become observant of the world around them and more aware of the life they are living. It serves as a low-risk place for student writers to experiment with words, sounds, and figures of speech; to become more conscious of the nuances of language; to engage in metaphorical thinking; to tap into the illogic and free imaging of the unconscious mind; and to begin to express their emotions and experiences in a more literary way—to look at themselves through the somewhat distancing lens of language.

Students sometimes find it hard at first to understand the difference between a notebook and a journal and to form the habit of notebook keeping. To help them, for at least the first half of the year I make regular notebook entries an assignment and give them plenty of suggestions for types of entries. My students write three or four entries a week. Some entries are assigned in connection with a particular work of literature being studied in class (see chapter 7 for examples) or with a specific aspect of poetry writing. Others may be selected from lists of suggestions, with an alternative choice of personal writing if there is something they really want or need to write about. Entries should always be labeled to identify the topic and the date of writing.

At the beginning of the year, at least, I collect the notebooks weekly, read through the entries, and comment on them. Comments on notebooks should for the most part be kept simple and personal ("I can really see this scene!" "Ouch!" "Wonderful images," "An intriguing list"); questioning, to generate more material (with an answer expected); and nonjudgmental, to encourage experimentation in the notebook. Suggestions for adding to or revising an entry are made lightly and with the purpose of helping the student work up an entry as a finished piece of writing.

A student's notebook grade is based solely on turning it in on time with completed assignments, although if the entries are becoming too brief and cursorily done, I may make thoroughness a criterion. Mechanics such as spelling and punctuation are not part of the grade. Unlike a journal, the notebook does not usually promote the most intimate personal outpourings, but if students have written something they do not want other readers to see, they can fold over the page and I will not look at it. Of course, I am suspicious if this happens too often.

I always want to read through the entries every week and comment on them. But busy English teachers facing stacks of student writing often don't have the time to read and comment on piles of notebooks weekly. Once, torn between what I knew was a good generative writing activity for the students and my own lack of time, I found some other ways to deal with the notebooks. As is so often the case in teaching, the solutions to a problem had advantages I hadn't even thought about: Broadening the audience for the notebooks encouraged better entries, enthusiasm for writing entries grew, and students got ideas from each other. Young writers often get excited about some of their entries (especially the more outrageous fictions) and want to read them to their peers; this can spur a class competition in entries. Emulation and competition can be great motivators!

I like to alternate among the following ways of having the writers' notebooks read (whichever method I choose, I make sure writers still retain the right of privacy with any entries they don't want to share).

- Devote ten or fifteen minutes of writing group time to reading and commenting on notebook entries, either by reading entries aloud or by passing the notebooks around for silent reading. (The writer may choose which entry to have read.)

- Let each student read one entry aloud to the class, or have writing groups choose one to read to the class.

- Have students exchange notebooks with each other for written comments.

- Have two students read chosen entries aloud to each other. You may ask whoever reads an entry to initial and date the reading.

- Ask all your students to write the same entry in class (particularly entries to go with literature you are reading) and read them in groups or, if your class is small enough, read the entries around the room.

- Have students revise one entry; you read the original and the revision for comment.

- Have students mark one entry for you to read and comment on. Or you might choose one entry to read.

- Read some students' entries one week, some another.

- Read nothing; just check to see that students have done the assignment.

- Look at some notebooks during class while the groups are working.

- On an irregular basis, collect the notebooks and read all the entries.

I use the notebooks in a number of ways. During the writing workshop period, I encourage students to go back through their notebooks for ideas. Some entries become finished pieces; other provide ideas, images, or phrases for another piece. If a specific assignment has been given on a piece of literature, the entries may be used during class to enrich discussion. Periodically publishing excerpts from the notebooks for the rest of the class to read can stimulate greater efforts and give students ideas for their writing. Which entries to publish should always be the writer's choice. I give each student one sheet of paper on which to copy any entries he or she wants and to decorate in any way. Then I just photocopy the pages to make a booklet for each member of the class.

I prefer not to call this notebook a journal because most of my students identify that word with a different kind of journal keeping. However, the word *notebook* can sometimes be confused with their academic note-keeping. I talk this over with my students and let them choose a name; usually we just call it the "Writer's."

NOTEBOOK TOPICS

The lists of writer's notebook ideas that follow are some that I give my students to help them think of things to write about. The lists suggest the kinds of topics that work well in the writer's notebook. Students enjoy writing these entries, which are meant to increase verbal facility and observation and to stimulate students' imaginations. I don't give the entire set of lists to students at one time but present the class with a new list about every two weeks. They may choose topics from any of the lists they have accumulated or write about an observation, thought, or event of their own. Students are great at coming up with additional topics to include in the lists.

Collecting

1. Listen to people talking and collect at least five strange comments or accidentally funny remarks.

2. Make a list of things you have lost or misplaced. Put a checkmark in front of the ones you wish you still had. Add to the list any items that have mysteriously disappeared. If you want, describe one object and/ or its loss.[1]

3. Make a list titled "My Favorite Things." Include all kinds of things: activities, food, weather, objects, colors, and so on.

4. Look around you during the week for visual oddities (for example, a glove wrapped around a tree or a Band-aid stuck to a stop sign). List at least five. Elaborate on one: Either describe it in some detail or expand on the thoughts it gives rise to.

5. When you notice something amusing, write an entry looking at the event or item from an unusual perspective—for example, a poem about scarves, gloves, or sleeves that are trying to escape from a locker.

6. Look around you for human interest: people doing odd, funny, or interesting things. Elaborate on one instance.

7. When you are in a car or the school bus, look out the window for vignettes of people that you find touching or funny. List at least five. Speculate on the circumstances of one.

8. Make a list of books you never want to read again, places you never want to go again, things you hope you'll never have to do again, food you never want to eat again, and so on.[2]

9. Make the opposite list from those in number 8: books, places, experiences, and so on that you would like to repeat.

10. Collect at least five quotations that have special meaning for you. They may be from books, songs, or poems.

11. List things in today's world that make you really angry.

12. Make a list of questions you would really like to have an answer to.[3]

13. Make a list of ways to complete the sentence "I wish I were...."

14. Make up at least five sayings you would like to find in a fortune cookie. Then make up five you would hate to find.

15. Make a list of memorable things that have happened in your lifetime (personal or public).

16. Make a list of things that have been invented in (a) your lifetime, (b) your parents' lifetime, and (c) your grandparents' lifetime.

17. Look up a newspaper or magazine from the month and/or year of your birth. Tell what was happening in the world at that time.

Observing Reality

1. Sit in one place for ten or fifteen minutes and write down everything you observe: sights, sounds, smells, feelings, colors, temperature, light, and so on.

2. Go back to the same place and observe again. Have any of the details changed? Do you observe more?

3. Go to a place you love or hate four or five times during the week at different times of the day. Take a few notes each time, and then write an entry that shows what intrigues you about the place.[4]

4. Sit where you can watch a group of people. Observe what they are doing with their time. Are any of them wasting time or fooling around? Define what *you* mean by "wasting time" or "fooling around." Might someone else define their activities differently?[5]

5. Overheard conversations: Write down as much as you can of a conversation between no more than two or three people. Be as accurate as you can in getting down the exact words.

6. Watch somebody doing something and try to describe that person's appearance and actions completely objectively, with no emotion or judgment on your part.

7. Look at an object you find beautiful, ugly, or interesting, and describe it so someone else can see it the same way you do.

8. Sit in one room and list the shapes you can find. Try to be exact in describing the shapes and the objects that create the shapes.

9. Sit in a public place (the library or the mall, for example) and list the different kinds of people you see coming and going. If you want, describe one person in detail.

10. Go for a walk and write down everything you see, hear, smell, and feel. Include the weather.

11. Observe one small neighborhood in great detail. Look at the size and shape of buildings; observe people; notice plant and animal life. What do you hear, smell, and feel? Describe colors, geometrical shapes, and activities in the neighborhood.

12. Describe to a blind person some sight you wouldn't want to lose. What sight would you most want to keep and remember? How would you describe that sight so it could be "seen" by someone else?

Observing Yourself

1. Pick two things that are important to you, two things that seem very dissimilar. Try to discover whether they have some quality in common that reveals something to you.

2. Analyze your moods: What are they like? What seems to bring them on? What are your recurring moods? What mood are you in now? Describe your mood, not just in general terms, but try to say exactly how you feel. Use metaphor or simile if that helps.[6]

3. Try to remember all you can of a particular event that occurred when you were much younger. Write about all the details you can remember.

4. What situations make you nervous? Try to analyze why. Are they situations that you think make most people nervous?[7]

5. Write about something you wanted very much—and maybe worked long and hard for—but were not able to get.[8]

6. Look at yourself in a mirror for as long as you can take it. Write about what you see.[9]

7. What, for you, is the difference between a good day and a bad day?[10]

8. Write an "annual report" on the state of yourself. Compared to what you were a year ago, what are you now? What do you plan or hope to be a year from now?[11]

9. Write a letter to yourself as you will be five years from now; ten years from now.

10. Write a letter to yourself as you were five years ago.

11. Right now, based on your experience, what practical information about life, living, and growing up could you give to a younger person?[12]

12. What pleased you today? What irritated you today?[13]

13. Notice your behavior on one day and describe it. As an "impersonal" third-person narrator, describe the person the behavior reveals.

14. What characteristics have been handed down to you by your family, such as attitudes, behavior, character traits, or looks? Where in you do you see your mother and father, your grandparents, or your siblings?

15. Write a "personals" advertisement about yourself.

16. Write a help-wanted ad that describes a job perfect for your characteristics.

17. If you could have a personality transplant, what would you want transplanted? Describe yourself after the transplant.

18. What is your greatest treasure? Why? Describe it so someone else can understand why it is precious to you.

Exaggerating Reality

1. Exaggerate something you did. Make it extreme![14]

2. Create a really convincing lie.

3. Change a situation you experienced to make it come out the way you wanted it to. Or change it to make it come out worse than it did.

4. Write about an event or part of your life as if it were a movie or play. Write a story about the event in the third person and show it as someone else might see it.

5. As a detached, disinterested observer, describe an event or incident you witnessed. Then pretend you were a participant and rewrite the description in the first person.[15]

6. If today were a meal, what would it be like? If today were a piece of music, what would it be like?[16] Continue to describe the day, creating your own categories.

7. After you have spent some time with someone, write about the experience, not as you experienced it but as you think the other person might have.

8. Write about tomorrow as if it were happening today.

9. Invent a wonderful dream and write it as if you really dreamed it last night.

10. Create a fantasy that fulfills a long-held wish.

Be sure to label all these entries!

Freewriting

1. Do an unedited five- to ten-minute freewriting, just spilling out anything that comes into your mind.

2. Do a focused freewriting, concentrating on a particular topic.

3. Do a "cluster" of words and phrases starting with an interesting word or topic you'd like to write about.

4. Circle one word from a previous freewriting and do another freewriting starting from that word.

5. Circle one word from a freewriting and do a cluster around it.

6. Do a freewriting chain of memories, letting each memory trigger another.

Bragging (Elaborate on Your Answer)

1. I am really very good at _____.

2. I really did a good thing when I _____.

3. I wish everybody would do what I do when I _____.

4. My best friend would say that I _____.

5. I would want my obituary to say that I _____.

6. If I were in charge of things around here, I would _____.

7. I know what to do about _____, and it's to _____.

8. What I like about my appearance is _____.

9. What I like about my personality is _____.

10. What I like about my character is _____.

11. What I have to offer the world is _____.

12. I am really pleased that I said _____.

Fictionalizing

1. Describe your pet. Then describe yourself, speaking as your pet.

2. You wake up to discover that you are someone else, or something else. Describe how you feel in this change and how you see life.

3. Taking off from a news story, describe the events from the inside, as if you were somebody involved. Use details to be convincing.

4. Create a dialogue between two people: It doesn't have to go anywhere or be conclusive. Try to catch the genuine speech sounds.

5. Make up conversation-stopping sentences, such as, "Has anyone seen that piece of cake I was saving?" or, "You're going to ask him to the prom? I thought he was going steady."

6. Invent a past for yourself. Make it colorful and convincing.

7. Create a list of inventions you think the world needs. Be outrageous and imaginative.

8. You are an alien seeing human beings for the first time. Describe them as you see them. What is your reaction to their appearance and their behavior?

9. Write a letter to an object you like, to something in nature, or to a historical person, a character in literature, or someone you know who has died.

10. Write a letter back from the thing or person in number 9.

11. Pretend you are the creator of a world. What would you create? (If you want, write in the form of the Bible: "Let there be ...")

12. Invite five famous people (alive or dead) to have dinner with you. What would the conversation be like? You could also invite five characters from fiction.

13. Invent a past for a character you read about.

Colors

1. Look for colors in the world around you. Try to find an object to match each of the following colors: white, gray, red, scarlet, crimson, pink, rose, vermillion, yellow, gold, orange, blue, azure, green, violet, purple, brown, and black.[17]

2. Look around you and find new names for colors you see in the room or outside. Invent new adjectives (not "sky blue" but something different) and new similes (not "red as a beet" but something new).

3. If you could change the colors of things, what would you make them? Why?

4. Make a list of colors to describe your moods, avoiding standards such as blue for sadness.

5. Describe people you know, read about, or see in terms of colors: Who is a "green" person, a "violet" person, and so on?

6. If sounds were colors, what colors would they be?

7. Do certain colors have a taste, a smell, or a texture?

8. What do you think of as your colors? Why?

Word Play and Naming

1. Find words that are interesting just for their sounds. List words that sound beautiful and words that sound ugly, without any relationship to their meaning.

2. Make a list of fifteen words you like, for whatever reason. Then combine some of them into crazy phrases and funny combinations. Or exchange lists with someone else and combine their words into phrases.

3. Start a list of new words you come across in reading, conversation, TV, movies, or elsewhere that interest you. Use these words in serious or funny sentences or phrases.

4. Collect palindromes (mom, kayak, a Toyota).

5. Create as many words as you can from the letters in your name. Write a joke or poem about yourself, using at least five of these words.

6. Look up the meaning of your name. Does it seem appropriate to you? Does it fit you? Why was it chosen? If you could choose your own name today, what would it be? Why?

7. Find as many words as you can that rhyme with your first name and your last name.

8. If you could rename your friends, what would you name them? Why?

9. What would you do if you had the chance to give all the creatures names? Give new names to some animals, flowers, or other natural phenomena.

10. What things in nature have names that sound just perfect to you? What ones are absolutely wrong? Why? What should the names be?

11. Groups of creatures have interesting words to describe them, such as litter of puppies, school of fish, pride of lions, and so on. Collect as many of these phrases as you can.

12. Invent names for other groups of creatures, such as a group of students, parents, teachers, siblings, and so on.

13. List five or more current slang words and write (a) a dictionary-style definition, (b) a synonym, and (c) an antonym.

14. Invent five or more new slang words and define them.

15. Describe what you mean when you say "beautiful," "ugly," "smart," "dumb," or other adjectives of the same kind.

16. Start a list of puns that you hear. Start a list of puns that you invent.

17. Take a simple verb such as *walk* and find words that include an adverb in their meaning (stroll, meander, etc.).

Interviewing

1. Interview your mother, father, or some other person older than you about the past. Write about what you learned in third person—or in first person.

2. Write a letter to an author, or write a list of questions you would like to ask an author in an interview.

3. Interview a character from fiction or from a movie or TV show.

4. Interview yourself.

5. Interview a famous or historical person.

6. Interview God to find out why certain things were put on Earth, or ask any other questions you would like answered. Be either serious or funny or both.

Figurative Language

1. Make a list of similes about yourself. ("My hair is like ...")

2. Make a list of metaphors about yourself. ("I am a ...")

3. Look around your bedroom, kitchen, or a room in the school. What objects seem to have personalities? Personify at least five. ("The telephone is hanging around nervously, holding its breath as it waits for an important call.")

4. Do the same thing as in number 3 and make a list of similes ("The telephone is like ...") or metaphors ("The telephone is ...").

5. Write five or more alliterative sentences, in which every word starts with the same sound.

6. Invent new hyperboles (exaggerations) to describe physical conditions: "I'm so tired I could ... ," "I'm so hungry ... ," "He's so gorgeous...."

7. Make a list of your favorite onomatopoeic words. Then use several of them in sentences or phrases.

8. Invent several oxymorons, such as "cold fire," "sweet sorrow," or "happy tears." Use two or more of them in sentences.

9. Take an abstraction (beauty, infinity, hate), a place (Chicago, France, Princeton), or a thing (the sky, your favorite pen, a piano) and write about it as if it were a person you knew very well.

10. Write in the voice of a personified object or abstraction. What would your piano say to or about you if it could talk? Would that be different, for example, the day before and the day after a recital?

11. Invent some new similes to replace clichés such as "slow as a snail" and "busy as a bee."

Jottings: Collections for the Writer's Storehouse

1. Jot down any unusual, striking, or interesting lines, phrases, or images that come into your mind as you are observing something around you.

2. Start a list of new words you hear, with their definitions.

3. Start a list of words that intrigue you for any reason or that appeal to you because of their sound or the connotations they have for you.

4. Begin a section to collect ideas for writing topics, taken from any source that gives you an idea: newspaper articles, memories, things you read, ideas from classes, or events.

5. Write down your dreams. You don't need to describe a whole dream unless you want to; just jot down images from dreams. Keep the notebook (or some paper) beside your bed so you can write the images down when you first wake up from a dream.

6. Start collecting vignettes or "slices of life" — pictures seen as you pass through life.

7. Start a collection of funny or provocative headlines from newspapers.

8. Start a collection of memories, especially through the images they evoke.

Remembering Childhood

1. A special outing — with the whole family or with mother, father, or another relative.

2. A store you often went to.

3. A friend you played with.

4. Kindergarten or nursery school.

5. Being sick.

6. A special Christmas, Hanukkah, or other holiday.

7. A secret never before revealed.

8. A food you loved or hated.

9. A special book.

10. A fear.

11. A place you have since lost.

12. A gift you gave.

13. A birthday.

14. The first day of school.

15. Moving.

16. Being treated as a real person instead of as a kid.

17. Being treated as someone special or important.

18. Listening: sounds, voices, words.

19. Learning to read.

20. Next door.

21. A disappointment.

22. A mysterious or unexplainable memory (people, place, or event).

23. Family stories, legends, or myths.

24. A new sister or brother.

25. Weather.

26. A special treat just for you.

27. An injustice.

28. Being taken advantage of because of your age.

29. The funniest thing you remember.

30. A lonely moment.

31. A neighborhood character.

32. A best friend.

33. An enemy.

34. A sibling.

35. A family vacation.

36. Your first time away from home.

37. A daydream.

38. A recurrent dream or nightmare.

39. Your earliest memory.

40. Performing for others.

41. A song.

42. Favorite or hated clothes.

43. Home: typical sounds, smells, colors, and so on.

44. Lessons.

45. Showing off.

46. Shopping (food, clothes, shoes, back-to-school).

47. Being cruel.

48. A haircut or hairdo.

49. Laughing or crying out of control.

50. Being mischievous or naughty.

51. A punishment.

52. The most wonderful present.

53. Something mean.

54. Being lost.

55. A special adult: neighbor, teacher, or relative.

REWORKING ENTRIES INTO POETRY

Periodically, I ask students to take a notebook entry and turn it into a poem. The following are some examples of poems written from notebook entries.

From "Overheard conversations":

Typical
alcoholic green Mondays when
Jamie ne pas stationner devant with
broken windows in
ten halls (such a
hard essay topic)
It's wrong but
lunch crumbs attract
ants and mashed men

like, like, likes are
absorbing heat but the
Braves give it away now to
JV freshmen with
purple hair
flying on CDs that just
Oh!
you know?

—Laura Fitton, Grade 10

From "If today were ...":

Tuesday, April 5, 1988

If today were a meal,
It'd be a bowl full of memories
that have gone stale,
and are rotting away.

If today were a shirt,
It'd be a tank top—
worn—in an old
yearning to be washed.

If today were a sport
It'd be sailing—
smooth yet rough,
warm and relaxing.

If today were an animal
It'd be a camel—
neverending with energy
but slow and brown.

If today were a place
It'd be flat and wide
dry with tall grass,
hard with angular rocks.

If today were a song
It'd have no words—
it would flow on gracefully
stopping for some jazz.

If today were a chair
It'd be a lifeguard stand
the color of wood
and topped with an umbrella.

If today were a book
It'd be poetry—
full of rhythm and beat
peacefully praising life.

If today were a shoe
It'd be a yellow flip-flop
unaware of the truth
casual and free.

If today were a pillow
It'd be hard and long—
Not wanting to be used
and without a pillowcase.

—Jennie Priory, Grade 10

From a dream image:

Nightmare

the external anxiety
of a mortal soul
with visions of fire and
demons that laugh
and here I am with wounds
in my heart, my hands and
my feet are being torn apart
screams around me whose
sounds never reach
I crawl and decide I am going
to escape, but jackals and snakes
are guarding the doors in agony

—Cristina Alvarez, Grade 10

From an entry about a pet:

Pumpkin (for my cat)

The sonorous notes of the birds'
songs
Send the messages to my ears.
Dove perched on my shoulder
whispers the love once given.
When will the blue jays return?
Why have they gone?
Please don't leave me without
your music.

—Najah Mas'udi, Grade 11

From a memory entry:

Catsleep

6:30 — Half-sleep and the Last in a series
      of dreams
      I made a sudden violent move with my leg —
      like the twitching animals make
      in that fleeting moment between
      life and death.

      The warm bundle of cat went over
      the side of the bed.
     A soft landing and
      he carefully reoriented and rearranged himself.
      Front paws dug deep in the carpet
      he arched and yawned.

7:00 — No cat food but he was content
      to lick the sides of the empty
      plastic yogurt container.
     Satisfied, fat Cheshire cat.

3:30 — Bus stopped — I looked up;
      the clouds hung oppressively low.
     It smelled like death.
     Garage door opened — dark and dank.
     The Devil visited the front stoop and
      left an opaque garbage bag.

4:00 — No sounds except for the faint sad melody
      of a piccolo.
     A hole in the ground near the junipers
     The soft warm earth and Tomb.
     I stopped to hear rain falling.

               — Julie R. Leegwater-Kim, Grade 12

From an alliteration entry:

You

Unmistakable Uniqueness You Unveil,
Understanding Underlies Unforgettable Upbeat,
Utilizing Your Undertow,
You Upsweep Uninhibitance,
Unglued — Utterly Unsurpassable —
You

               — Shelley Wollert, Grade 10

From a collecting entry on sensory detail:

Mocha and Coca

Purrr, Purrr
Scratch, Scratch, Scratch,
Meow, Meow.

Crackle of the fire in a cozy
    livingroom,
Mocha stretches out on the
    window sill near the
    fireplace,
Watching the snow fall.

The hypnotizing purr of Coca,
Curled up on the footstool,
She gently lifts her head,
The scent of a roasting turkey
    wafts through the room.

Meow, Meow,
Scratch, Scratch,
Purr, Purr,
Shhhhh ...

— Alma Moxon, Grade 10

From observing the details in a room:

Noticed

Shadows have enveloped most of the
    wall covered in wildflower wallpaper
    the floor
    the edges of the doorway at which the wall
    ends.

But
    an incandescent light diffusing some shadows
    leaks out from between hard edges of door and
    doorway
    through the gap
    into the
    silence of the dark
    room.

Tones of mirth escape occasionally from the
    bright, through the same ajar door.

The young child who grasps his knees to his chin
    and rests his back on the wall
    looks down, poutless,
    noticing.

— Liadan O'Callaghan, Grade 10

From a changed point of view entry:

Ant

Running, Stopping, Dodging the traffic
Hoping not to end up a Black Mess ...
   as the aftermath of a sneaker,
I run so fast I can't stop.
The towering green foliage in
   front of me is
Difficult to get through.
Running up, down, around.
Suddenly, a tremendous Shadow
   surrounds me
Run....

The rubber shoe squeaked on the
ground covering the silent scream—
All left is a black imprint.

       —Vivia Font, Grade 10

From an entry about sensory images:

Forest Fire

Rip
Six times
I wonder how many trees that took ...
Like a spotlight
Eyes focus on the curved piece of glass
With the shreds piled on top
Like the thin, curling smoke
From a German cottage in the
   mountains,
A chain of elegant puffs unwinds
The match touches a shred
It has begun
The glowing color of charcoal in the
   winter fireplace

Extends itself into an orange wire
Weaving itself around the edges
One, two ... , three ... , four, five ...
I look back
And the first has become but a black
   crinkle
Which crackles like the toasted skin of
   marshmallow
They are all like that,
Dead
And I am fascinated.

       —Shuko Kawase, Grade 10

NOTES

[1]Eric Kraft and Charles Neuschafer. *Personal*. Lexington, MA: Ginn, 1975, 111.

[2]Adapted from an idea in ibid., 126.

[3]Adapted from an idea in ibid., 30.

[4]Ken Macrorie. *Writing to Be Read*. Rochelle Park, NJ: Hayden Book Company, 1968, 147.

[5]Adapted from an idea in Kraft and Neuschafer, 122.

[6]Adapted from an idea in ibid., 126.

[7]Adapted from an idea in ibid., 136.

[8]Ibid., 154.

[9]Ibid., 14.

[10]Ibid., 30.

[11]Adapted from an idea in ibid., 37.

[12]Ibid., 42.

[13]Ibid., 92.

[14]Adapted from an idea in ibid., 115.

[15]Adapted from an idea in ibid., 129.

[16]Adapted from an idea in ibid., 174.

[17]Ibid., 130.

4 Getting Started

There is a basin in the mind where words
float around on thought and thought on
sound and sight.

— Zora Neale Hurston

There are several ways you can begin poetry writing with students. My preference is the "take it easy" approach: Just start right in without much—if any—introduction, always after the class has been reading poetry, so they have it in their minds and ears. If the teacher approaches poetry writing casually and matter-of-factly, without a big announcement, students are doing it before they know what hit them. Almost all students really do enjoy writing poetry once they have begun, and it seems sensible to start them out without fanfare and with the expectation that they will like it. When they are hooked, they can be drawn into the subtleties of technique and revision.

If, however, you know you are going to face negative reactions to poetry writing, or if when you start you discover such reactions, it may be better to confront the students' attitudes head-on. One way to do that is to have them write in their notebooks about their feelings, answering such questions as, "What do you think of when you hear the word *poetry*?" "List some words that come into your mind in association with poetry," or, "Describe an experience you have had with poetry." For various reasons, some students are afraid of poetry; others think it's not "cool" to enjoy it, and certainly wouldn't be caught dead writing it! Let students have their say: It's important for you to understand their attitudes and prejudices. Then discuss their comments in class. Your own responses should be low-key and nondefensive. You can talk simply about why you read and write poetry, but don't try to convert the unconvinced all at once.

I usually don't introduce poetry writing immediately in the school year. I do start the writer's notebook right away, handing out the lists "Collecting" and "Observing Reality" the first or second week, and "Observing Yourself" and "Exaggerating Reality" the next. After that, I give the class a new set of topics every week or two, reminding them that they are adding to, not replacing, lists: They can use any topic they haven't done yet. At the same time, I begin the poetry reading component of the class, not in a separate "unit on poetry," but more casually. I like to read and discuss poetry often; for example, while students are reading a novel, I devote some class time to poetry. At this early stage we don't do heavy analysis or explication but look at a poem in the reader response vein, simply talking over what we enjoy about it and what it means to us. I ask students to bring in favorite poems, read them aloud, and talk about them. Only after they have grown used to poetry reading in the class, have done some other writing, are comfortable with their writing groups, and have accumulated notebook entries for at least three weeks do I introduce the poetry writing program.

The best way to defuse poetry writing hostility, should you encounter it, is simply not to force poetry at first. If someone is really against the idea, don't insist; let that student do the assignments as prose. Later, when the fear of poetry has dissipated, students can always reshape prose pieces into poems. When the class becomes involved and students begin reading their poetry to each other, the reluctant ones usually find they want to join in, and in some of your assignments they will be writing poetry without being particularly conscious that they are.

If you prefer to begin poetry writing with formal considerations about poetry put in a more academic context, you might start with a freewheeling discussion of the questions "What is poetry?" and "What is a poem?"—two questions that arise very naturally when you are reading poetry with a class. First, brainstorm responses to the questions, writing on the board or on graffiti paper without comment, and then open each idea for discussion. You could ask the class to look for poems that support or disprove each contention. To what extent does a poem need rhythm and rhyme? What does a poem look like on the page? Does the wording of poetry differ from that of prose? These questions are not easy to answer, and it is likely that no conclusive answers will emerge, although the class might come up with a working definition. You may decide that definition is not yet possible. At this point a class is often interested in considering some statements about poetry that have been made by poets themselves and questioning their accuracy (noting the many contradictions):

> *Poetry is the spontaneous overflow of powerful feelings ... emotion recollected in tranquility.*
>
> —William Wordsworth

> *Poetry is not a turning loose of emotion, but an escape from emotion; it is not the expression of personality, but an escape from personality.*
>
> —T. S. Eliot

> *Poetry is the art of uniting pleasure with truth.*
>
> —Samuel Johnson

> *Out of a quarrel with others we make rhetoric; out of a quarrel with ourselves we make poetry.*
>
> —William Butler Yeats

> *If I read a book and it makes my body so cold no fire can ever warm me, I know that is poetry.*
>
> —Emily Dickinson

> *A poem is a fresh look and a fresh listen.*
>
> —Robert Frost

> *[Poetry is] the movement from overclothed blindness to a naked vision.*
>
> —Dylan Thomas

*Let us understand by poetry all literary production
which attains the power of giving pleasure by its
form, as distinct from its matter.*
　　　　　　　　　　　　　　—Walter Pater

*What is poetry? The suggestion, by the imagination,
of noble grounds for the noble emotions.*
　　　　　　　　　　　　　　—John Ruskin

... imaginary gardens with real toads in them....
　　　　　　　　　　　　　　—Marianne Moore

Poetry is life distilled.
　　　　　　　　—Gwendolyn Brooks

You should be sure to end, at least, with the conclusion that poetry is neither an arcane mystery nor limited to the Great Works of Undying (but dead) Authors.

Now assign three or four poems, of different kinds, to read—both free verse and poems that follow various poetic forms. In their notebooks, have students write a brief personal response to each poem (not a formal analysis) and list the questions about poetry the assignment raises.

In class: Read the poems and talk about them in any way the students want. Discuss their questions, and keep the questions on a sheet of paper on the bulletin board to refer back to or add to.

Assignment: *Find a poem you like to read aloud to the class. Write in your notebook specifically why the poem appeals to you. Practice reading it aloud.*

If you haven't previously talked about how to read a poem aloud, this is the time to spend a few minutes doing so and to begin an ongoing thread of the class: oral interpretation of poetry. In class the next day, have students read the poems aloud and talk about their reactions.

TWELVE BEGINNING LESSONS

Whichever approach to introducing poetry writing you have chosen, the following suggestions may be useful in getting students started on their writing. The twelve lessons described here are arranged to ease young authors in, to let them understand what makes poetry writing interesting, and to bring up elements of poetic technique gradually rather than all at once. Each lesson begins with one or more prewriting exercises—reading, talking, or writing—to help students understand the assignments and to generate ideas for imaginative poetry. The notebook assignments for a lesson may either replace regular weekly entries or be done in addition to them.

The whole poetry writing project should move by easy stages: Make it seem natural. Let students warm up first and enjoy assignments done throughout the year, rather than giving one massive poetry writing unit and then going on to something else. However you work, it's best to avoid two extremes: the formalist approach of having a class write only poems copying standard fixed forms and the laissez-faire approach in which students can spill out anything and have it count as poetry.

Lesson 1:
Using Interesting Words

Poetry is language surprised in the act of changing into meaning.

—Stanley Kunitz

I find that starting from the stimulus of language, rather than from the personal, is a valuable way to begin poetry writing, because it is not threatening to the wary. For many students, this approach will allow a freedom to try poetry without exposing themselves and their feelings too nakedly. It gives them a chance to experiment with words, relax the rules, and start being poetic under the guise of being silly. And it invites the possibility of weird and wonderful language use. I like to open with a consideration of the English language and its wealth of words in any context, not just in poetry.

Assignment: *Bring in to class two lists of words: the ten most beautiful words in the English language and the ten ugliest—by sound only. Try to blot out what the words mean, and listen only to how they sound.*

In class: Have the students write their words on two blackboards or sheets of newsprint: the beautiful words on one, the ugly on another. Put in some of your own favorites of both kinds. Then talk about what elements in the words seem to make them either attractive or unattractive. Why is *pandemonium* so euphonious when its meaning is "a wild uproar"? Why does *crepuscular* sound unpleasant when twilight is lovely? Discuss disagreement among students; one's beautiful word might be another's ugly.

Obviously, in exercises like this, you have to know what to expect from your particular class and adjust the activities accordingly. If your group would be likely to indulge heavily in obscene or offensive language, you might regulate the outcome by such devices as writing on the board yourself or having them hand in their words for you to photocopy—or maybe you'd want to use this chance to address issues of offensive language use and levels of language.

Ask students to write a poem or a prose paragraph using at least five of the beautiful or ugly words. Tell them not to think about form. They might write a narrative, a vignette, a description, a list of metaphors or similes, or total nonsense. Then have them share what they have written. A good technique at the earliest stages of poetry writing is for you to collect all the writings, give them a good mix, and then read them aloud anonymously, honoring each effort with your best sincere poetic reading. This not only avoids the beginning writers' embarrassed giggling; even better, it startles both authors and audience to hear their work read seriously and discover how good some of it can be. I have found that serious reading increases students' respect for poetry writing, for their class-mates, and for themselves. Read the poems without comment, except about the words. Talk about what the words do in the writings; ask the class to point out striking and unusual phrases, either appealing or repellent.

Sometimes, before you ask students to write, especially if they are somewhat shy of it, beginning with a class poem can make the writing a fun, comfortable, social activity. Have the class compose a poem together while you write on the board what they decide. Or writing groups might work together to write collaborative group poems.

The following poems exemplify a variety of student responses stimulated by lists of beautiful and ugly words.

Atmosphere

Light falling rain; dawn
moon-lit dew droplets sleeping on turquoise swirled
    sapphire petals
White button stars strewn across a black velvet sky
pearly satin and liquid silk trickle down jagged
    metal icicles under white light
snowflakes of odd wicker shapes float, soar,
    topple, dash on top of ice
dream-hearted nymphs with woven heather crowns
    dance amid sharp crags by the pure ocean
    of jade
morning

                —Suzanne Arcuni, Grade 10

Aura

Scintillating and svelte,
Glitzy and glamorous,
A luscious smile played upon
Her sultry lips.
Her eyes danced in the moonlight,
A soft zephyr swept up wisps
Of her raven black hair.
The burgundy velvet of her dress
Blended with the night.
An orchid was tucked behind one ear.
A strand of pearls encircled her neck
Her cream-colored skin
Contrasted with the black sky.
An aura surrounded her figure
... The shadows by the sea-side stood
    enraptured.

       —Asra Saleem, Grade 10

Smirk

The dour smirk
looked like
mildew on
an urban sewer.

    —Danielle Vaughan,
        Grade 10

Anarchy

At Drumthwacket
Stigma is fluent

Anarchies of comucopias
Are ambiguous lineaments

Arrays of ullulations
Soliloquy the charisma
Of iridescent appendectomies

Fahrvergnugen flourishes
In pomegranates of faldfees

Pajamas can be pumpernickels

Cordial duodenums

Claim melodious
Opalescence

Annihilated holocausts
Snap arrogant solar plexes

—Laura Fitton, Grade 10

Lesson 2:
Simile

*Poetry ... the mysteries of the irrational
perceived through rational words.*

—Vladimir Nabokov

*Poetry is enthusiasm taken through the prism of the
intellect and spread on the screen in a color, all the
way from hyperbole at one end ... to understatement
at the other end.*

—Robert Frost

Simile and metaphor are probably the most commonly used figures of speech in poetry. Both figures imply a kind of analogy, showing a relationship or making a comparison between two, often dissimilar, things. An early grasp of what these figures mean and their essential function in poetry will help students not only write more interesting poems from the beginning, but also start to understand the nature of poetry. I start teaching poetic analogy with simile because many students already know the term, and those who don't are quick to learn that it is a figure of speech comparing two dissimilar things that uses the word *like* or *as* to make the comparison specific.

In class: Discuss the meaning of the term *simile*. Give the students some examples, such as "I'm as hungry as a bear," "My love is like a red, red rose," "Red as a rose is she," "Very like a whale," and "Your teeth are like the stars (they come out at night)." Extend the list with students' contributions of other similes they are familiar with.

Then practice inventing similes together as a class. Try to make your similes extreme, even crazy, but apropos. Start by suggesting something outrageous and discuss why it describes effectively. First as a class, and then as individuals, have students complete similes such as the following:

I love you like ...

The sun burst out from behind the clouds like ...

The moon last night looked down like ...

Rain moved across the yard like ...

The students left the classroom like ...

Waves came in on the beach like ...

If the class wants to do more, let them come up with the first part of other similes. Compare their finished similes and see how differently they describe the same phenomenon. What varied attitudes toward the thing do they express? How are similes able to show an attitude or emotion without actually telling what it is?

Notebook assignment: *Do a simile entry from the "Figurative Language" list in chapter 3.*

In class: Read some of the similes aloud to the class.

Optional assignment: *Take one simile and extend it into a longer, more detailed description, in either poetry or prose.*

the touch of a fingertip
as easy as a lion's kiss...
—Sian Killingsworth,
Grade 12

Sweat clings to the forehead
like a thin layer of honey.
—Shuko Kawase, Grade 10

Lightning lit up the dark sky
Like a peacock displaying its
feathers.
The stallion raced like a ghost
Into the storm
As an insect is drawn to a
spider's web.
—Karin Seminack, Grade 10

Jazzy

Sitting in a nightclub I look into
your eyes as they sparkle with the
electricity of lasers.
We listen to the smooth-as-silk
jazz in the smoke-filled club.
The high notes of the trumpet sting my ears
like a loud screech.
The words you say to me
are like the electricity in ultra-violet lights.
You whisper,
"I love you,"
and it stings my heart.
—Joy Robinson, Grade 10

The Opening Dance

<pre>
                    Life is like
dancing
                    only your partner
                                    may be
Luck
                    Chance
                                or Fate.
                    Be careful
that your toes
                    are not
                                stepped on
for
                    sore toes
                                make it difficult
to walk.
                    Let the rhythm guide
you
                    although I can't
guarantee
                    there
                                won't be
a few jerks
                    or
                                ill-guided
steps
                    along the way
</pre>

— Jane Lee-You, Grade 11

Lesson 3:
Creating Metaphor

*Poetry begins in trivial metaphors, pretty metaphors,
"grace" metaphors, and goes on to the profoundest
thinking that we have.*

—Robert Frost

Metaphor reveals similarities between things in an implied comparison without using the word *like* or *as*. One of the most fundamental poetic elements, metaphor is a way of condensing, of seeing afresh, of expressing ideas and feelings without spelling them out, and of transmitting the indescribable. One value of metaphor is defined by Ron Padgett: "By taking our feelings, which are sometimes unclear to us, and finding an object or an action that expresses them, we sharpen our understanding of ourselves and can pass that understanding on to people who have similar feelings."[1]

An excellent beginning exercise to help students understand and create metaphor is described in the booklet "Creative Writing: A Manual for Teachers" by Toi Derricotte and Madeline Tiger Bass.[2] As I unfold the exercise to the class, I help students by starting each step on the board with the whole class first, before they do it individually; the class poem serves as a model for their own. Have each student do the following steps.

On a sheet of paper, write a list of abstract nouns, such as "love, beauty, anger, justice," in a column. Next to it, write another list, of colors. Use some unusual color names, such as colors modified by a striking adjective or colors from an artist's palette. Then make a third list, of concrete objects, such as "shoe, river, ring, roller coaster."

Next, draw a line that connects an abstraction on the first list to a color on the second and then to a concrete object on the third. Continue connecting words on the three lists. Don't try to be logical; let the imagination run free and find odd and intriguing connections.

Now choose one of the combinations you've created and write it as a metaphor: "Jealousy is a black car." Then add a second line beginning with *that* or *which*: "That drag-races with love." Finally, add a third line beginning with *and* or *but*: "But never wins."

Jealousy is a black car
That drag-races with love
But never wins.

—Paula Gonzalez, Grade 11

Pride is a snake-black fingernail
That grows and curls
Until it becomes ingrown.

—Liadan O'Callaghan, Grade 10

Imagination is a magenta bird
free to fly wild
afraid to fly home.

—Christina Jimenez, Grade 10

This exercise is a good way to help students understand metaphor and to have fun creating metaphors. Some students will want to extend the poem they write.

A Peacock Green Freedom

Obsession is an indigo blush,
a surfacing anger that won't give up,
Twilight shall be my flicker of persistence,
sharpening, until time will make obsession dwindle,
Magenta grandfather clocks turn my dreams into nightmares,
A whistle of cucumber reminds me of your giggled profile,
beauty can be a winterwhite key,
locking down an indigo blush,
and gripping obsession tighter,
a forest green thickness of whoever will be next,
so I can't let go

—Shelley Wollert, Grade 10

Lesson 4:
Subjective Metaphor

*A poet is not an author, but the subject of a
lyric facing the world in the first person.*

—Boris Pasternak

Creating metaphors about themselves usually intrigues young writers. The
following exercise is somewhat circular: It helps students understand metaphor
by letting them express their feelings about themselves, and their self-perceptions,
in a roundabout way, and it simultaneously helps them understand themselves
better through the creation of metaphor. Read and discuss Sylvia Plath's poem
"Metaphors," in which she lists metaphors for her pregnancy in nine nine-syllable
lines.[3] Raise questions such as: How does she describe being pregnant? What
emotions does she reveal? What attitudes toward her condition do the metaphors
convey? What wider meaning do you understand from her metaphors? What is
the effect of including a variety of metaphors, from the beautiful to the
ludicrous, from highly unusual imagery to common expressions?

Assignment: *Choose a characteristic of your own. It can be a physical or
mental trait, an interest, or a particular temporary condition such as having a
sprained ankle. Make a list of between five and ten metaphors to describe the
characteristic. Include one or two clichés or adages if they seem to add interest to
your list.*

Incognito

I am a riddle
vision on a platform
traveling to another world incognito.
an undercover cop on a painted set
moon exerting as much light as it can on faithful bystanders
a pms woman full of large emotions
showing them all.
You can get a headache when the lights of my home
flash on so quickly after I say farewell.

—Christina Jimenez, Grade 10

I am a coat of many colors
Red, hot, fire engine,
Blue, windy day,
Bright, yellow daisy in the sun,
Dark, dull, grey cloud
Blissful, white stream,
"Black Death."

—Soyoung Bethea, Grade 10

I'm Information Central.
A source of entertainment.
The wine with everything always in
   motion.
The Bell invention permanently in use.
A radio that is never turned off.

—Sharon D'Mello, Grade 10

Field Hockey

I'm a tornado flattening a row of houses
A buzzard hungrily watching out for its prey
A fire burning a path through the field
A Roadrunner speeding with a coyote on its tail
A golfer hitting the ball for a hole in one.

       —Jennifer Cornew, Grade 10

     At a thoughtless carefree moment,
     I'm speeding through life on a runaway rocket,
     And times are changing, but not
     always for the better.

       —Kim Gentempo, Grade 10

Lesson 5:
Observation and Metaphor

*I do not think anybody ever knows the discreet
use of metaphor, his own and other people's,
the discreet handling of metaphor, unless he
has been properly trained in poetry.*

       —Robert Frost

Writing poetry helps students become more conscious of observing the world around them and of finding unusual ways of seeing. This lesson is intended to encourage them to discover odd similarities between disparate things by modeling a poem on Ricardo Pau-Llosa's poem "The Red Hole,"[4] (see p. 64). I'm always amazed at the comparisons it evokes.

In class: Read and discuss "The Red Hole." What is Pau-Llosa describing? How and when do you know? Look very closely at his choices of comparisons: Are they all alike, or are they different? From what areas of life are they drawn? How do they make you see—and react to—the moon? What is the effect of keeping the word *moon* out of the poem until the last line?

The Red Hole

A burning rose,
the cupped palm of a martyr,
a flamingo crushed by a truck,
a bite-mark on the throat,
an apple-bloodied eyelid, a copper
penny like a drop of frozen blood,
a Revlon-red-cell
whose mitosis is speech,
whose nucleus is a kiss,
a quark, a neutron, a button,
a chalice, a red postmark,
a cut bone, a petal,
a beachball glowing like a lit stove,
a period in red ink on a student's paper,
the heart's comma, a drawer knob,
a rusty keyhole, a drop of acid on skin,
a round flame, the sliced artery of a corpse,
ringworm, the eye of a moth, an open
parachute, the rope-burn of the sky-diver,
a target, a bullet hole in the temple
an arrow through the wrist, the wax
seal of a letter, a stop-light,
a hole left in a cheek by a laser beam,
the sun setting or rising, a fingerprint
in blood, a digital-clock zero, a nipple,
a fiery magnet, a blood sample through
a microscope, the hole left by a pulled molar,
a fertile ovule sliced in half,
a tear in Caesar's robe,
the horizon moon, March 6th, 11:34 PM, on the beach.

Notebook assignment: *Bring in the statement "(a) looks like (b)" about something you observe, as in Pau-Llosa's implied "The horizon moon looks like a red hole." The first element should be something very specific that you have observed: the moon, a snake, or the Milky Way. The second element should describe its appearance in general terms: "the snake looks like a black belt" or "the Milky Way looks like a pearl necklace." Then make a list of other things that have the same shape (and color, if appropriate) as item (b)—the red hole, the black belt, the pearl necklace. Try to include both appealing and unappealing items, the beautiful and the ugly.*

Ricardo Pau-Llosa's "The Red Hole" appears in *Sorting Metaphors* (Tallahassee, FL: Anhinga Press, 1983; © Ricardo Pau-Llosa) and is reprinted with permission.

In class: In a small class, ask students to write their lists on the board; then have the class go around and add other suggestions (if you know your students will be neither obscene nor cruel). In a larger class, use writing groups to expand the lists. Have students in each group pass around their lists for additions.

Assignment: *Write a poem modeled on Pau-Llosa's, using (b) for the title and ending with a flat statement of the original observation. Consider the ways the items on your list combine and contrast with one another. Choose from your list the items that most suggest what you want to say, and decide what order is most interesting.*

The Black Belt

a withering string
stem of a flower
the neck of a vine
an oblong finger or toe
an I-V
spiral staircase
horizontal sunset
a chain earring
crooked Venetian blinds
thread hanging from a sewing needle
a piece of hair floating in the
   atmosphere
the fallen strap from a pocket book
the fringes that sway from a
   Hallowe'en costume
a broken shoe lace
Dreads in the summer
overgrown fingernails
the hands in the face of a clock
bristles from a broomstick
worn mop strings
a broken arm
yarn hanging from a sweater
gold chain bracelet
kitestring in the wind
a satisfied leech
a stream of spilled coffee
chocolate syrup being poured
dental floss
the stream of blood from a gash:
a garden snake, Oct. 7, 8:30 p.m.
in the yard.

—Paulett White, Grade 11

The Pearl Necklace

A row of teeth
A dozen eggs
White frozen peas
Frozen droplets of rain
Drops of milk on a black table
Pieces of chalk on the ledge of a
   blackboard
Buttons on a silky blouse
Snowballs before a playful fight
A charm bracelet
The spine
Old ice cubes in a tray
Pebbles
Corn on the cob
Segments of a worm
The bottom side of your toes
Rattle of a rattlesnake
The teeth of a clam
White Christmas lights in the dark
Dandruff or lice in a head of hair
Wild mushrooms in a forest
Rice Krispies in a dark chocolate bar
White blood cells
Snowflakes falling during a storm
White polka dots on a black shirt
The lights on an exquisite chandelier
Broken pieces of shell on a beach
A rib cage
Maggots
Fried grease that's been sitting in a
   pan overnight:
The Milky Way, seen through a
   telescope, on the 8th of March,
   10:40 at night.

—Helina Rheem, Grade 11

Waltzing Bugs

Dust in my eyeglasses,
Black glitter glue
in blond hair, Fish food
swimming in aquarium seas,
The space in the weave of white linen,
Absent-minded pen dot doodles, Printed
words on dull texts at midnight,
The reverse effect of reflected light,
Pepper on pale
scrambled eggs, The Summoner's seething
carbuncles, Dirty hail storms,
Spattered mud on rabbit fur, Crumbs of devil's
food cake on white paper plates,
Black swiss-dot lace pantyhose,
Goofy goggle-eyed stickers, Poppy seeds
on a kaiser roll, Dripped dots of molten black wax,
A page full of missing i dots,
Black beans in white cream soup, Ebony nailpolish
chippings on an ivory desk,
Fallen lenten ashes, Four
thousand one hundred and forty dilated pupils,
Ginseng tea leaves in my cup at two A.M.

—Sarah Taylor, Grade 12

Clock

A moment on the move
A rhythmic DANCE
hands in motion
Encircling time
a numerical succession
step to the beat
dissection of life
turning ahead
a fall back
Spinning deliriously

—Amy Hunter,
Grade 12

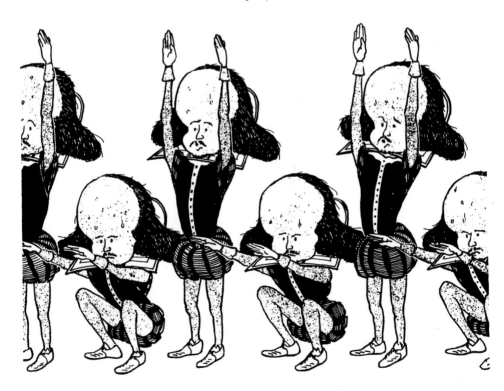

Lesson 6:
Some Writing Tips

The lunatic, the lover, and the poet
Are of imagination all compact.

— William Shakespeare

By now, your students are writing poetry, whether they know it or not. This is a good time to introduce, lightly, a few basic concepts to keep in mind while they are writing. Spend at least part of a class period discussing the following ideas. You might illustrate with some good examples from what the class has already written and from published poetry.

1. "Show, don't tell." Contemporary poetry tends to shy away from sentimentalism, direct expressions of emotion, and heavy philosophical explanations of ideas. Looking at two or three contemporary poems, help students consider the importance of letting the imagery of a poem create meaning and of being very concrete in images. The poet should never have to explain the meaning of a poem in the poem. This is a concept that will need continual reemphasis for most writers.

2. Poetry should surprise in some way. Try to avoid cliché (word combinations or phrases that you have heard over and over). Break out of the expected grooves. Ask the class to look through their notebooks and mark some entries they think contain elements of surprise. (This might be a good time for a class collection of snippets from notebook entries.)

3. Poetry should have integrity. The parts of the poem should work together, and the form of the poem should fit with what it is saying.

4. Poetry does not have to be (a) serious, (b) an expression of deep feelings, (c) pretty, (d) "poetic," (e) profound, or even (f) completely understandable. It does not have to "mean."

A poem should not mean,
But be.

— Archibald MacLeish

Lesson 7:
Images

*In writing poetry, you're interested in condensation,
so you don't try to put all of a particular impression
or inspiration on a single page. You distill. Poetry is
life distilled.*

—Gwendolyn Brooks

An image is the presentation in words of a strong sensory impression, a physical sensation. Images can convey sight, sound, touch, odor, or even taste. It's through learning to create strong images that students will be able to show and not tell. To help them understand the role of images in making their writing come alive, spend some time asking students to notice and record images of the ordinary, the elements of their daily lives, and help them find such images in published poetry.

Notebook assignment: *Do either number 1, 2, 10, or 11 from the list "Observing Reality" in chapter 3. Or think of a moment in your recent experience that is memorable for small reasons (neither the best nor worst moment in your life); remember and write in your notebook all the details you can about that moment.*

In class: Read and discuss a poem that works primarily through presenting images, such as Robert Bly's "Driving Toward the Lac Qui Parle River."[5] Look particularly at the sensory elements in the poem. How do images depict the moment of experience itself and also show how the writer feels?

With the class or in writing groups, read some of the notebook entries on images and discuss the sensory details that are most effective. Ask each other questions to elicit more detail.

Assignment: *Write a poem that describes the event or observation you wrote about in your notebook, using sensory detail (images) to make it come alive for a reader and to convey your feelings about the experience without naming them.*

Summer Night

The darkness is thick
and muffling.

The moon through the screen is large,
reflecting in the ocean
an endless beam of white.

Lying between the cool sheets
I perspire.

Surf pounds the beach,
then withdraws.

The night insects hum
only when I listen.

A salty breeze off the ocean
feathers my skin so softly,
and I shiver.

—Elizabeth Moxon, Grade 11

My Grandmother's Kitchen

A glass teapot
upon a brown stove—

Sounds of
passing cars,
footsteps
on the pavements—
greeted
by white curtains,
blown back
and forth.

An open
newspaper
under a cup
of coffee
near a plate
of doughnuts—
chocolate, lemon,
cinnamon, cream—

And
on the wall—
between
the windows—
a hushed
cuckoo clock—
Still,

at the turn
of the hour.

—Carin Companick,
Grade 11

Released Peace

The fleshy, pink balls of my feet
Smoothly brush along the
Harsh, weather-worn grey deck.
They tap monotonously and unconsciously.

The moon, full, and watching
Over the ocean on the horizon
Seems paused
And content in solitude.

I am absorbed in my familiar surroundings—
Rusty beach chair, warm, salty sweater.
My body has finally stopped its nervous rituals
And the fingers of the cool air touch my skin—
Lightly and softly ...

—Tara Jones, Grade 11

Lesson 8:
Writing Poems About a Memory

*Poetry is the art of understanding
what it is to be alive.*
—Archibald MacLeish

Memories provide one of the richest sources of material for all writers. This lesson is designed to elicit memory as a basis for student poetry writing.

In class: Do the following memory writing exercise (based on an exercise from James Moffett and Betty Jane Wagner).[6]

1. For ten minutes, have students freewrite, in their notebooks, a chain of memories, letting each memory trigger another. (Demonstrate aloud: Begin by looking around you and letting something start you off, and then list a chain of memories, not lingering on any one: "— reminds me of — which reminds me of — which reminds me of — .") Remember that freewriting doesn't interpose an editor, and its purpose is only to spill out ideas; don't stop and worry about punctuation, spelling, or grammar. The only rule of freewriting is that you cannot stop writing. In this exercise, you don't need to put in the "reminds me of."

2. After as much discussion of the freewriting as seems appropriate, ask students to read their writing silently and then isolate one memory they would like to write about further, by circling a word or phrase that triggers a response when they see it on the page. The memory should focus on one incident, experience, or moment ("the afternoon I almost drowned"), rather than a long period ("the summer I was ten"), and preferably should be at least a year old.

3. Do a second freewriting (five to ten minutes), this time starting with the word or phrase each student circled, to focus on the specific memory. Before they start, suggest that students try to put themselves back into that moment and remember sensory impressions: what they saw, heard, felt (physically), smelled, and tasted; the weather; colors and light; what other people were around; and any other details they can recall. Have them write without stopping or editing, trying to get down as many details as possible.

4. Ask students to look through the freewriting and circle all the sensory images. If they don't have many images, suggest that they call up the memory again and try to see it, writing down what they see. Or they could describe the scene to a partner who would write down the details and ask questions to elicit more images. At this point, you might ask students to isolate the single detail that is most interesting or evocative to them, and then do a third freewriting starting with that detail.

Assignment: *Write a poem about your memory, perhaps starting with the detail you chose from the second freewriting. Try to let the reader in to the moment through sensory impressions. Don't tell too much about your feelings; show what they were.* (If some students really don't feel up to writing this as a poem, let them do it in prose, following the same rules. It can be turned into a poem later.)

In class: Read the poems aloud in groups and talk about how vividly the memory is reproduced. Some elements of the poem to discuss include:

*   What sense impressions were most vivid in the poem? Where would you like to see, hear, taste, smell, or feel more?

*   Where in the poem does the author *talk* about sensations or emotions and where are you allowed to *feel* them through the images?

- Are there enough details to re-create the memory? Is there anything to be cut: anything that doesn't fit or that tells too much?

- Has the writer used interesting words and images to convey the memory? Has the writer avoided cliché?

- If the author has used figurative language, is it striking?

Sheheme

Under the floorboards
He and She lie next to me
face down
as the clomp of the Adults' feet
goes by above us.

Plates clink, clatter
as the waves resound.
A fork drops above us
We push our noses to the sand
not wanting to be found,
suppressing giggles.
Hidden under the section
where only adults may eat
"No Kids Allowed — Adults Only."
We wonder why.

If we look up
through the cracks
we'd see the brightness
and the dark-soled shoes,
and the sand would tumble
into our open eyes.

Looking ahead,
we crawl silently.
The grains go by under us
and push ahead in tight spots
where we squish through
and get sand between our teeth.

— Clare Gardner, Grade 12

Memory Book

i saw the lifeblood
of a july painted sky
streaking down the drain
of a december drowned
evening
in the click and hiss
of your dry silk voice
i hear stolen kisses
on a moist day
with the wind
licking and biting at my ears
i know that if i closed my eyes
i could clearly see
sunflowers swaying
your eyes rainbowed in exuberant
      carbonation
this daylight is tender
and dissolving
in my fingertips
but you catch the deluge
in your teeth
and somehow we're on
the front porch, sultry july
at forbidden midnight
you search my fractured eye, i can't
cross to the mirrorland
on the other side of the iris
i twist in kaleidoscopic patterns
in shades of rust
in the palm of your hand
like water down a sink

— Sian Killingsworth, Grade 11

Mrs. Davison's Hands

They made such perfect letters
They cut and pasted so well.
They always cleaned up, too.
I always wondered how come no one
      ever gave
Mrs. Davison's hands
A gold star.

        —Stephanie Truesdell, Grade 12

My Mother Hates These Trees

I went to Disney World and Mickey Mouse came to visit.
I had to do my timed tests in three minutes.
I longed to be the star on the Bulletin Board.
I wore my pink jumper, sat in the park, and got bored.
I looked at my pictures of shorts and ponytails.
I could finally reach the doorbell.
Mrs. Nieto made us clean our cubbies very well.
Mrs. Conlan scolded me for not finishing my homework.
Mrs. Hiltz scolded me for not finishing my homework.
My mother scolded me for making tennis balls out of toilet
      paper.
My mother hated everything about those paper balls—my
      masterpiece.
My mother thought the fir trees blocked the sun and
      brought too many bees.
My mother hates these trees.

        —Mai Abdala, Grade 10

Lesson 9:
Poetry Poker

*I look for the forms
things want to come as*

*from what black wells of possibility,
how a thing will
unfold ...*

        —A. R. Ammons

One of the delights for a poetry teacher is helping young writers break through convention and learn to make imaginative leaps in language, imagery, and idea. "Poetry Poker" is a great way to ignite creative sparks. This game, which was introduced to me by poet and teacher Lynn Powell, is a favorite with my students.

Make a deck of index cards with one word written on each card, primarily nouns, some verbs, a few adjectives (especially colors), and almost no adverbs. Be sure both common and unusual words are included. These words will form the basis for a poem.

In class: Students each draw five cards from the deck, and after looking at the set of five they may exchange any card for a new one. They must keep the words they receive in the second draw. Then each student writes a poem that contains all five words. It could be any kind of poem: a list of similes or metaphors, a narrative, a bit of description, or total nonsense. Words may be used in any grammatical form — for example, nouns may be used as verbs or verbs as nouns, adjectives may be changed to adverbs, and so on.

Sometimes it helps to begin the game with a class poem. In a more advanced class, you can have students pass their set of cards to another person after the first poem has been written and then compare the two poems, which most likely will be utterly different. The comparisons should not be evaluative but appreciative, focusing on the different slant each writer took.

I keep my deck of poetry poker cards in my desk drawer to pull out if there should be a few minutes left at the end of a class or as a reward for extra hard effort and concentration on the work of the day. Of course, I don't do this too often, so the game will remain a treat.

Beyond the pyramid

As they draw closer to us, now just beyond
    the pyramid one can see their crimson
    robes billowing on the desert sand
    like stray apples on a cornfield.
Silence, save the rhythmic beat of their
    age-old drums rising above our short
    hastened breath,
The dark shadows of their copper shields cast
    on the sand — the absolute reversal
    of the peaceful stars
    like droplets in the sky.

          —Suzanne Arcuni, Grade 10

Desire

desire
perched on a balcony
longs
for life below
bored with
angels
yearning for
felons
under the stump
of the earth

          —Laura Fitton,
          Grade 10

Skaters

The pond is new crystallized and slick, like smoky glass.
The children slip down the hill,
Their feet, covered in moccasins,
Tap the surface as if asking a vital question.
Answered, the moccasins are discarded
Like a used skin and replaced.
They skate excitedly,
The blades clashing like a saxophone
Over the lacquered lake.

          —Stephanie Schragger, Grade 10

Lone Orchard

Sitting in the lone orchard
and eating my red apple, I sensed an
   overpowering force.
A force whose home
was the giant mountains,
a violent force I knew to be a hurricane.
Just when I was about to leave,
a thin, drawn-out wind
like the song of a flute
met my ears.
Then
a silver raindrop fell
and glistened on my red apple,
glistened with magic.
I stayed.

—Helen Payne, Grade 11

The Power of a Book

Opening the book
Opens the hypnotic seesaw
And sprigs
of the tusk mind.

—Vanita Gupta, Grade 10

The Fisherman

The fisherman stands on the seashore —
silently he sees
the gray clouds
staring at the water,
like a woman
admiring her mirror-reflection
He watches the water scurry
across the stones
and then hurry

back to the ocean —
teasing the sand
keeping its secret.
The hurricane
is heralded
by the first drops
of rain
and scolding thunder.

—Caroline Sheerin, Grade 10

Lesson 10:
Mistranslation

I've written some poetry I don't understand myself.

—Carl Sandburg

Another way to shake students loose from conventional language and imagery is to ask them to "translate" from a language they don't know. Pass out two or three poems written in another language, such as German, Spanish, French, Latin, Russian, or Anglo-Saxon. Have students choose one from an unfamiliar language and "translate" it, using only the appearance and sounds of the words to make a loose but poetic approximation of what they see or hear. The poems don't have to make any sense; students can make their own meaning from impressions of the original. They can translate word by word, line by line, or in any way they want, and they don't have to adhere slavishly to the forms of the original. As they translate, the writers may find that the poem begins to take on a life of its own; by the end of their writing, it usually has moved away from the original text to become their own poem. The poems are often funny, interesting, and sometimes quite moving or deep.

When I do this exercise with my students, I have them work on the poems in class; then I collect the finished poems and read them all aloud, giving them my most serious and dramatic oral interpretation. This makes for a hilarious ending to the class period and provides a real sense of the joy of working with poetic elements. At the same time, I take the opportunity to repeat and comment on the beauty of one unconventional line or phrase from each poem. My students leave class both laughing and saying to each other, "We're really good! I can't believe it!" A good source of poems for mistranslation is Stanley Burnshaw, ed., *The Poem Itself* (New York: Simon & Schuster, 1981). Some examples of "translations" of Friedrich Hölderlin's "Hälfte des Lebens" follow.

Hälfte des Lebens

Mit gelben Birnen hänget
Und voll mit wilden Rosen
Das Land in den See,
Ihr holden Schwäne,
Und trunken von Küssen
Tunkt ihr das Haupt
Ins heilignüchterne Wasser.

Weh mir, wo nem' ich, wenn
Es Winter ist, die Blumen, und wo
Den Sonnenschein
Und Schatten der Erde?
Die Mauern stehn
Sprachlos and kalt, im Winde
Klirren die Fahnen.

— German poem by Friedrich Hölderlin[7]

Some student poems written as "translations" of Hölderlin's "Hälfte des Lebens":

Song to the Free

My brother went away
And took with him a wild rose,
To the land of sight
Where swans hold their places in the water
And doves, inebriated by the sun, fly forever,
All are as happy as can be.
The intellectuals wallow in their books.

Where am I, what place is this
Where winter sets in, and blooming flowers die,
And where there is no sunshine,
And nothing to warm our hearts?
I want to go to my brother
Where the wind blows and sparrows sing,
To the land of fantasy.

— Maritza Maxwell, Grade 11

Its golden body hung
Wrapped in wild roses,
Hanging for all to see
From its open suitcases of time.
Hope tangibly flowing out
Our trip is beginning.

Through mire, brush, and fen,
Where winter blows, and trees ever
     bloom
Under the shining sun.
And this is the Eden
From the beginning of Time
Salt and pepper spread with the breeze
We're killing Mother Nature and
Ending Father Time.

—Seema Chowdhury, Grade 11

My gazelle buried a hatchet
And found a wild rose.
From the land to the sea
He threw it. It hit a swan.
As drunken as a monkey,
He packed his trunk full of honey
And hang-glided to Warsaw.

With a mirror to locate his itch, he
     scratched.
In the winter he died of frozen blue
     skin
And we all sang him a sonnet.
Did our voices shatter glass?
His mother was stern.
She scolded and called in the wind.

—Ellen Cottone, Grade 11

The Things I Have to Do

I must hang up my clothes
I must weed the Rose garden
Sometimes it's hard to see
Why I'm held to these tasks.
I must unpack my trunk
My trunk full of memories
Some things are lonely.

When everything is over I must do something
In the winter even when the roses are dead
Black and lifeless
Why must I always?
Even after death
There are things I must do
And when I die?

—Lorena Sayer, Grade 11

This kind of imaginative response to the sound and visual aspect of a foreign language loosens the writer's unconscious mind through free associations and relieves students of the responsibility of coming up with an idea of their own. When you (or they) read the "translations" aloud, ask the class to look out for surprising images, fresh expressions, funny bits, interesting mysterious lines, thought-provoking or teasing phrases, and metaphors. Talk about surprise and the fact that poetry can intrigue when it is not too literal. Even when the whole poem doesn't work, many will contain amazingly evocative lines, such as these from a recent sophomore class:

The dead move stern Spreading like salt in the wind — Shelley Wollert	I mourn for these dead dreams I threw the pieces into the wind — Alma Moxon
Doesn't your voice cry at the age of flowering — Sharon D'Mello	this winter of woe that blooms from sunshine through green shutters — Liadan O'Callaghan
and wear the robe of the sun porpoise — Christina Jimenez	a hand which spills the soil is a hand of perfect life — Michelle Evaul
and the sea will be a great thing between us — Jennifer Cornew	there is no living without a chance to relive — Shuko Kawase

You could extend the exercise by asking students to write a new poem, choosing one line from the "translation" and using it as the first line of another, totally different poem.

Lesson 11:
Cliché

Poetry is like fish: if it's fresh, it's good; if it's stale, it's bad; and if you're not certain, try it on the cat.

—Osbert Sitwell

Most of us find it easiest to say things in ways we have heard before. Cliché is always a problem for student writers, and it will need to be discussed more than once during the course of the year.

In class: Begin by emphasizing the positive, looking at the role played by fresh images and metaphors in making poetry interesting and alive. Read together a poem such as Dylan Thomas's "Fern Hill" for some examples of ways to subvert old familiar phrases ("happy as the grass was green," "all the moon long") and invent new ones ("fire green as grass," "my sky blue trades").[8] Discuss the fact that many of our most common idiomatic expressions were once bright new ways of looking at the world—for example, "eager beaver," "red as a beet," "break of day," "a beehive of activity," "falling asleep." Now they have become so commonplace that we don't even think about their origins in imaginative imagery.

Define cliché if necessary and elicit a few examples. Give students time to think of several clichés and write them in their notebooks. Then put some clichés on the board; look at them together to see how the originally powerful poetic devices have become tired and have lost their significance.

Notebook assignment (or group work in class): *Rewrite five or six clichés so they have a new force.* (It may be useful to do some examples first with the whole class when you give the assignment.)

In class: Have students write their new phrases on the board or read them aloud from the notebooks. Discuss what makes the new expressions fresh, not cliché. If you want, write a class or group poem incorporating several of the new expressions.

When you comment on student writing, try to avoid criticizing a poem by labeling clichés as such. You can achieve the same result by mentioning that you have heard the idea expressed like that before and suggesting that the writer try to find a fresher way of saying it. In my classes, we talk about the way common expressions "wear a groove" in the brain, so that if you hear them, you don't have to think about what they mean. A reader cannot be intrigued or startled by a new idea expressed in a well-worn phrase. When one of my tenth-graders used the phrase "drifted off to sleep" in a poem, we began to wonder how many other verbs could be used to express the different ways of falling asleep. I asked the students to bring in as many new verbs as they could think of, and the next day they listed well over a hundred different verbs to connote the kind of sleep to come, with such suggestions as "evaporated into sleep," "waltzed off to sleep," and "careened into sleep." It was a good illustration that there are still new ways to express old ideas.

Lesson 12:
Persona Poem

Poetry is the supreme fiction, madame.

—Wallace Stevens

Student readers and writers of poetry often become confused about the distinction between the speaker of a poem and the author. To what extent, even in writing about an actual event, does the author add, delete, or change facts in transforming experience into art? One way to help students realize that truth in poetry does not have to mean the literal transcribing of experience is to ask them to assume a narrative voice that is not their own. In the persona poem, the author takes on the character of another person (the "persona") and writes in that person's voice and perspective. Persona poems include dramatic monologues, which imply a spoken address to a listener; interior monologues, in which the narrator's thoughts are recorded; and epistles, letters from the persona to someone else.

In class: Read at least three of the wonderful persona poems that you can find in most poetry anthologies. Some suggestions are Robert Browning's "My Last Duchess," "Soliloquy of the Spanish Cloister," or "Porphyria's Lover"; Alfred, Lord Tennyson's "Ulysses";[9] Ezra Pound's "The River Merchant's Wife: A

Letter";[10] Sylvia Plath's "Daddy" or "The Applicant";[11] Anne Sexton's "Unknown Girl in the Maternity Ward";[12] Gwendolyn Brooks's "We Real Cool"; and T. S. Eliot's "The Love Song of J. Alfred Prufrock."[13] Talk about the poems and how the character of the persona is created through speech.

Notebook assignment: *Choose a persona in whose voice to write. This might be a character from literature or the movies, a historical figure, a sports hero, or a politician. The persona could be someone you know or it could be entirely imaginary. It might be another person in a poem we have read in class. It could even be your own alter ego. Write a long diary entry in the voice of your persona. Explore the persona's character and inner thoughts about a particular situation, event, or person in its life.*

In class: Read the diary entries with the writing group. Ask questions to clarify the nature of the persona and to elicit more detail about the persona's character and personality.

Assignment: *Write a persona poem assuming the voice of the character you have chosen. You may choose to write in the form of a dramatic monologue, an interior monologue, or an epistle (letter).*

In class: Read the poems in writing groups, focusing the discussion on the techniques each writer used to bring the persona to life and how fully the character has been developed. Because students in this assignment are writing in an assumed voice and not their own, this is a good poem with which to have them practice oral interpretation: Give everyone a chance to read the poem aloud to the rest of the class.

Alone at Sunrise

With bags under my eyes
And messed up hair
I shuffle off to work
Alone at sunrise
With only my shadow as company
The cloudy gray pebbles crunch
Beneath me
I heavily sigh
Clenching my worn coat
around my aching shoulders

I can hear the blackbirds
greeting me
The big brick house
appears in the distance
So pretty, so proper
As I walk on the porch,
I wipe the wet from my face
"Mornin' ma'am" I say
"Nice day out today"

—Wiley Nelson, Grade 12

Raymond

Course there aren't any bookshelves.
Course I have no books, yeah.

I definitely, definitely have to be in bed by eleven,
Course lights out at eleven.

Who's on first?
Do you take any prescription medication?

I just see things,
246 toothpicks, yeah, definitely.

Course Monday night is Italian night.
Course I definitely, definitely need my cheese balls
    and my apple juice, yeah.

I want to learn how to dance,
Course I have a date at ten, got to be in bed by eleven.

Definitely, definitely
Two for good, one for bad.
Yeah.

—Shilpa Rustogi, Grade 12

Now launch out on assignments and lessons of your own, based on poems you encounter or on the literature the class is reading, on what is going on at school, on what happens in a particular class period, or on ideas the students themselves have. The more you work with poetry writing in your classes, the more you will find yourself inventing lessons and assignments on the spot. For example, when my students listed such a rich store of "sleep" verbs (mentioned in lesson 11), I asked them to write a poem starting with falling asleep in one of the ways they had invented and continuing with a description of the dream they might have from that kind of sleep.

Dreaming

As I floated into sleep,
my mind went rushing back
to the time when I lost my raft
    at sea.
The waves were pulling at my
    confused head,
they were trying
    to kill me.

As I ran on the white horses trying
to escape the evil spirits beneath,
I stumbled and hit my head hard,
    against what ... I don't know.

My mind was swirling in a mass
of oblique uncertainty. My consciousness
    was no longer with me, I
    could feel my uncleansed soul
        being pulled down to the
            depths of hell.

—Rebecca Owen, Grade 10

Chapter 6, "Creating Poetry Writing Topics," offers numerous suggestions for ways to develop topics for your class, as does chapter 7, "Writing About Literature Through Poetry." The annotated bibliography lists some books that are additional sources for poetry ideas. Chapter 5, "Teaching Poetry Writing," contains many more ideas for lessons to help students develop both technical skill and a deeper understanding of poetry. Remember that poetry exercises and assignments don't always have to yield finished poems but are ways of strengthening thinking and writing of all kinds.

NOTES

[1]Ron Padgett, ed. *The Teachers and Writers Handbook of Poetic Forms.* New York: Teachers and Writers Collaborative, 1987, 118.

[2]Toi Derricotte and Madeline Tiger Bass. "Creative Writing: A Manual for Teachers." Trenton: New Jersey State Council on the Arts, undated.

[3]Sylvia Plath's "Metaphors" may be found in X. J. Kennedy, *An Introduction to Poetry.* Boston: Little, Brown, 1971.

[4]Ricardo Pau-Llosa's "The Red Hole" may be found in *Sorting Metaphors.* Tallahassee, FL: Anhinga Press, 1983. First printed in *Kayak*, January 1982, no. 58.

[5]Robert Bly's "Driving Toward the Lac Qui Parle River" may be found in George Perkins, Scully Bradley, Richmond C. Beatty, and E. Hudson Long, eds. *The American Tradition in Literature.* New York: Random House, 1985.

[6]James Moffett and Betty Jane Wagner. *Student-Centered Language Arts and Reading, K-13.* Boston: Houghton Mifflin, 1981.

[7]Friedrich Hölderlin's "Hälfte des Lebens" may be found in Rosellen Brown, Marvin Hoffman, Martin Kushner, Phillip Lopate, and Sheila Murphy, eds. *The Whole Word Catalogue.* New York: Teachers and Writers Collaborative, 1972.

[8]Dylan Thomas's "Fern Hill" may be found in Helen McDonnell, John Pfordresher, and Gladys V. Veidemanis, eds. *England in Literature.* Glenview, IL: Scott, Foresman, 1987.

[9]Robert Browning's "My Last Duchess," "Soliloquy in a Spanish Cloister," and "Porphyria's Lover"; and Alfred, Lord Tennyson's "Ulysses" may be found in ibid.

[10]Ezra Pound's "The River Merchant's Wife: A Letter" may be found in Kennedy.

[11]Sylvia Plath's "Daddy" and "The Applicant" may be found in Perkins, Bradley, Beatty, and Long.

[12]Anne Sexton's "Unknown Girl in the Maternity Ward" may be found in Anne Sexton, *The Complete Poems.* Boston: Houghton Mifflin, 1981.

[13]Gwendolyn Brooks's "We Real Cool" and T. S. Eliot's "The Love Song of J. Alfred Prufrock" may be found in Kennedy.

5 Teaching Poetry Writing

True ease in writing comes from art, not chance,
As those move easiest who have learned to dance.

—Alexander Pope

For a good poet's made as well as born.

—Ben Jonson

Too often student poets believe that writing poetry is a matter of spilling out their emotions in any way and are sometimes reluctant to work on crafting their poems. That's understandable, because crafting is hard work. But good poetry writing requires close attention to matters of style, form, and diction. It's not true that just anything can count as poetry: Criteria for good poetry writing exist just as they do for good prose writing. This chapter offers suggestions for teaching some of the technical elements of poetry writing, with exercises to use with your class. Writing groups should consider any or all of these concepts when they are discussing their writing and when they are revising.

LANGUAGE

Language is called the garment of thought:
however, it should rather be, language is
the flesh-garment, the body, of thought.

—Thomas Carlyle

Poetry demands economic and exact language, fresh and appropriate wording. Analyzing good poetry will show students that poets are extraordinarily careful in choosing their words; even a poet like Walt Whitman, who on first glance seems to have written freely and loosely, has a reason for everything he does and has both selected words meticulously and revised extensively. Close attention to diction, syntax, and grammar is essential for good poetry writing, and students who internalize this knowledge begin to apply the same standards to the language of their prose as well.

Poetic Diction

A poet is, before anything else, a person who is passionately in love with language.

—W. H. Auden

Beginning writers often think there is a separate language of poetry and that certain words are innately "poetic." But poets may use words from many areas of life and levels of language. The following exercises are meant to help students see that the words of poetry can be widely varied.

1. Ask students to list words that they consider "hot" or "cold" on what I once heard Kenneth Koch call the "poetry thermometer."[1] You can do this either by having students generate the words themselves or by preparing a list of words you have taken from actual poems and asking the class to rank them from high to low on a scale of poeticism. Discuss the list: Are any of the words totally inappropriate in poetry? Why or why not? What might happen if the words at either extreme were used exclusively? What if they were mixed in the same poem? Under what circumstances can surprising words or combinations of words be effective? When might they lose their power, be inappropriate, or go too far? Challenge stock responses such as, "*sweat* would be inappropriate in a love poem."

2. Have students write a class poem using very "poetic" words: Go all out and see what happens. Then revise the poem. Try mixing; try using all "unpoetic" words. Come up with a version the class likes best. Challenge the choices they have made; make the students articulate why they have chosen or rejected certain words. If they end in disagreement, so much the better: You have begun a dialogue about diction (word choice) that can continue throughout the year.

3. Show the class several poems by authors whose poetic diction differs widely. Include William Shakespeare's sonnets, poems by John Donne, Percy Bysshe Shelley, or John Keats;[2] Emily Dickinson; passages from Whitman's *Song of Myself* or Allen Ginsburg's *Howl*; and Sylvia Plath's "Daddy" or "Death & Co."[3] Discuss the diction: How appropriate are the words the writers used in their poems? Could the words of different poems be interchanged? If so, to what degree? Is one kind of writing better or more poetic than another?

These exercises aim at two results: first, to sensitize students to the importance of careful word choice in their writing and, second, to help them understand that although there are no words that cannot be used in poetry, the diction of a good poem corresponds to and helps enact its meaning.

Strong Words,
Surprising Words

*Poetry teaches the enormous force of a few
words, and, in proportion to the inspiration,
checks loquacity.*

— Ralph Waldo Emerson

*The word-coining genius, as if thought plunged
into a sea of words and came up dripping.*

— Virginia Woolf

Student poets, not unnaturally, tend to use words and combinations of words that they have seen in poetry before. It's well worthwhile to spend some class time looking at language that makes the reader sit up and take notice of what's going on in a poem: the unusual choice of word or juxtaposition of words, the tautness of good poetry from the elimination of unnecessary words, and so on. To help students understand the impact of word choice in poetry writing, try the following exercises with a whole class or with writing groups.

1. Take a poem that you think has particularly effective diction and blank out some of the words. Ask the class to supply the missing words. Discuss their guesses and compare them with the poet's, to see how the writer chose words to create a particular meaning. Some of the students' choices may be exciting and fitting, too; use this opportunity to stress the variety possible in poetry and its nature as idiosyncratic personal expression.

2. Present a false version of a poem in which you have substituted some different, inappropriate, words for the author's; see if the class can pick out the words that do not fit.

3. For advanced classes, the poetry of Emily Dickinson is rich material for scrutinizing poetic language. Give the class a version of one of her poems with blanks where Dickinson had considered and rejected a number of different words; show students a list of all the words she had thought of using.[4] Discuss the connotations of the words and why she may have considered them; then talk about why she chose the one she did.

4. Have students each choose a poem that seems powerful to them in the way it uses language and, after they list favorite words in their notebooks, read the poems aloud in the class or in writing groups to initiate a discussion of effective diction.

Registers of Diction

Time ... Worships language and forgives
Everyone by whom it lives.
                        —William Butler Yeats

Look at several poems and analyze how the language of the poem affects its meaning. From what areas of life are the words drawn: common household activities, the law, medicine, or science, and so on? Are the words simple, monosyllabic, and Anglo-Saxon, or are they more elaborate, polysyllabic, and Latinate? How do these choices help the poem achieve meaning?

Compare, for example, the words in the opening stanzas of two American elegies, Phillis Wheatley's eighteenth-century poem "To His Excellency George Washington":[5]

> Celestial choir! enthron'd in realms of light,
>   Columbia's scenes of glorious toils I write.
> While freedom's cause her anxious breast alarms,
> She flashes dreadful in refulgent arms.

and the contemporary poem "The Leap" by James Dickey:[6]

> The only thing I have of Jane MacNaughton
> Is one instant of a dancing-class dance.
> She was the fastest runner in the seventh grade,
> My scrapbook says, even when boys were beginning
> To be as big as the girls.

Notice how the first poem's reliance on words with Latinate roots (underlined) elevates the tone and raises the subject above the reader and writer, whereas the simple, daily language of the second, with predominantly Anglo-Saxon roots, invites the reader into a common experience with the subject and the writer.

Most contemporary American poetry uses common words and imagery, but not all earlier poets relied on elevated Latinate constructions. Emily Dickinson for example, gained great force in her poetry by the tension between cosmic emotions and the diction of daily life:[7]

> Putting up
> Our life—His Porcelain—
> Like a Cup—
> Discarded of the Housewife—
> Quaint—or Broke—

> The Bustle in a House
> The Morning after Death ...
> The Sweeping up the Heart
> And putting Love away ...

The words Walt Whitman uses in *Song of Myself* derive from all walks of life and from both Anglo-Saxon and Latin roots. This inclusive use of language creates, in part, the inclusivity that he is trying to establish in the poem:[8]

> Out of the dimness opposite equals advance, always
>   substance and increase,
> Always a knit of identity, always distinction, always a
>   breed of life ...
>
> To elaborate is no avail, learn'd and unlearn'd feel that
>   it is so.
> Sure as the most certain sure, plumb in the uprights,
>   well entretied, braced in the beam,
> Stout as a horse, affectionate, haughty, electrical,
> I and this mystery here we stand.

Connotation

Great literature is simply language charged
with meaning to the utmost possible degree.

—Ezra Pound

Students sometimes use very odd words in their writing when they take synonyms from a thesaurus without considering the connotations of each word. Because it is derived from more than one root language, English is very rich in words, and along with the denotation or dictionary definition, every word carries its own set of connotations, associations that suggest something beyond the simple meaning. Consider the different connotations of the words *house* and *home* or of *dead*, *defunct*, *late*, and *passed on*.

Look at the connotations of words chosen from various sources. Take a poem such as Emily Dickinson's "There is no Frigate like a Book" and compare the connotations of her choices—*frigate*, *coursers*, *traverse*, and *chariot*—with the simpler words *ship*, *horses*, *journey*, and *cart*.[9] What did she gain from the connotations of her words?

Parts of Speech

Poetry is all nouns and verbs.

—Marianne Moore

Examine some modern poems for the way various parts of speech are used. Notice particularly the kinds of nouns, verbs, and adjectives, and the scarcity of adverbs. Any anthology that presents contemporary American poetry will have a large number of poems for you to use. Some I find particularly useful are Robert Bly's "Driving Toward the Lac Qui Parle River,"[10] Elizabeth Bishop's "One Art,"[11] A. R. Ammons's "Cascadilla Falls," Adrienne Rich's "Necessities of Life," and William Carlos Williams's "The Young Housewife."[12]

Ask the class to look carefully at each poem: What parts of speech predominate? What effect does that have? Is there a difference in poems dominated by nouns, verbs, or adjectives?

Revising for Language

> Prose: words in their best order; poetry:
> the best words in the best order.
>
> —Samuel Taylor Coleridge

Ask students to take one of their own poems and, with the writing group, look closely at all the language. Where is the diction particularly good? Where might they strengthen it? Where could they substitute a surprising word or change a weak verb (especially *to be*) for something more powerful? Where could they omit an adverb by using a verb that contains the meaning of verb and adverb— and often more? (Good examples are *amble*, *stroll*, *saunter*, *shamble*, or *dawdle* instead of *walk slowly*.) Where is the language out of place with the rest of the poem? Where do registers of diction collide? Where might they improve the poem by cutting out unnecessary words?

It sometimes happens that, in revising, students take fright at their most original and striking words and images and want to move toward a more conventional choice. This is a good time to suggest the danger of overworking and over-"poeticizing" a poem: Sometimes the writer's original word may be the more effective one.

Figurative Language

> And as imagination bodies forth
> The forms of things unknown, the poet's pen
> Turns them to shapes, and gives to airy nothing
> A local habitation and a name.
>
> —William Shakespeare

Poetry is highly figurative, and student writers and readers should become sensitive to the use of figurative language in poetry. Now and then you can ask the class to stop and look at figures of speech, in students' writing as well as in the literature you are reading. For the average class, don't be too heavy-handed in defining the figures and analyzing how they work. That can turn figurative language into a tedious academic exercise divorced from the students' own writing. Use the terms for the most common figures casually and comfortably so students see them as very natural and imaginative ways of expressing ideas, not as esoterica.

Playing with figures of speech is a pleasure for most students, if they are not confined to defining and identifying figures in other people's work. The notebook is a good place for students to do some experimenting with figurative language; several of the topics suggested in chapter 3, "The Writer's Notebook," have such a purpose. I find that my students, given a choice of assignments from various lists, will almost always do all the topics that deal with figures of speech.

IMAGES

*Poetry should be great and unobtrusive ... it
should strike the reader as a wording of his
own highest thoughts, and appear almost a
remembrance.... The rise, the progress, the
setting of imagery should, like the sun, come
natural to [the reader].*

—Percy Bysshe Shelley

Images live at the very heart of poetry; for students to write well, they must
understand the use of images. Contemporary poetry particularly depends on the
depiction of scenes, events, emotions, and thoughts through the senses. Young
writers need plenty of practice in creating images and combining them in interesting ways.

Show, Don't Tell

*When I see what you see, the distance
between us disappears.*

—Miguel Algarin

The following assignments are devised to help students remember the motto
of contemporary poetry, "Show, don't tell." A writer should try to put the reader
into an experience or scene and transmit emotion directly through the experience,
rather than describing the emotion itself.

In class: Look closely at images in the poetry the class is reading. Help
students actually visualize the pictures a poet creates and experience a poem
through all the senses the writer engages. Walt Whitman is an astonishing
exemplar of sensory image writing, and any of his poetry provides a rich basis for
examining images. "There Was a Child Went Forth" is a particularly good poem
in which to discover the impact of vivid visual images.[13] Students might want to
emulate Whitman's way of creating autobiography by simply presenting what the
child saw and heard in the world around him.

Notebook assignment or in-class exercise: *Generate a series of concrete
images and write them down in your notebook. For example, think of a specific
moment when you knew you felt sad (or glad, or furious, or in love, or any other
emotion). Describe everything around you at that time. Include details of the
place you were in: sights, sounds, smells, touch, weather, colors. What objects
around you seemed in sympathy with your feelings? Don't tell how you felt, but
let sensory images re-create your emotion.*

In class: Read the images from students' notebooks in writing groups and see
whether the group can identify the emotion associated with each image. Discuss
how the best images convey emotions without naming them. Which images are
most effective? Do any images seem to have gone too far (into sentimentality, for

example)? Which images seem ambiguous in describing the emotion? Is that ambiguity necessarily bad? When might you want to be ambiguous? When do you want to be perfectly clear?

Notebook assignment or in-class exercise: *Think about a movie or a particular part of a movie that conveyed a special emotion to you. What images did the filmmaker use to make you feel that emotion? Remember sound as well as pictures. Write the images down in your notebook.*

Notebook assignment: *Sit somewhere quiet and conjure up mental images. They can come from your life; from photographs, movies, or TV; from your reading; from dreams; or from your imagination. Let the images rise seemingly at random and write them down freely. Don't edit as you are doing this, and don't try to be "literary"; let your mind work like a camera, and simply record the pictures that come into it.*
Now look at your list. Is there any connection between the images? If so, write a poem using connected images. If you don't see a connection, take one image and elaborate on it. Or write a poem that connects disparate images in unusual ways.

Combining Images

There in the ring where name and image meet ...
—W. H. Auden

Every now and then, take some class time to help students come up with really unconventional visions and unusual ways of saying things. One good way of doing this is to combine images from a variety of sources. For example, generate unusual class lists of images to serve as springboards for poems:

- While you read several poems aloud, have students write down memorable phrases. Then list the phrases on the board and ask students to write a poem using a number of them.

- Take two or three images from each student's notebook (a variety of entries) and write them on the board.

- Assign a "walk around your neighborhood" entry and list images from various observations.

- List images from dreams.

- If students go on field trips, make observation of sensory details an assignment, and then draw up a class collection of images.

When a recent sophomore class was going to take a class trip to an art museum, I gave them a notebook assignment to look carefully at one picture for at least five minutes and write down images that came to them during that time.

When they came back, we listed on the board some phrases they particularly liked from their entries, and then they wrote poems containing those phrases. You could do the same thing with pictures from books or magazines.

False Mirror

As I gaze into the false mirror,
A menagerie of blue criss-crosses comes into my mind.
Hidden eyes watch me in the palace of true visions.
I wonder how I lost the coral pink serenity that I enjoyed.
What happened to the pastel flowers that gave me happiness?
I look up into the abstract sky for the answers but
    all I see is a brightness that is not gentle
    to my eyes.

          —Sharon D'Mello, Grade 10

Sky Room

Walk into the abstract sky
    room
The serene coral pink will reflect
    the idea of calm
Visions of bouquets of breakfast
    will fill the mind
Where skulls fit together and
    hidden eyes flow into each
        other
And the laugh can hear its peacefulness,
And the stubborn its reason,
In every space there is a menagerie
    of false mirrors which smile
        wisely ...
And battle the foolish of the
        mind.

        —Vivia Font, Grade 10

The Starry Night

a menagerie of hidden eyes
and in them, breakfast shapes
like instantaneous crisscrosses
of morning sunlight
dances of the skull
across abstract curtains
through this empire of true visions
the laugh
only with the first navy blue of the
    season

        —Shuko Kawase, Grade 10

Purely Images

A menagerie of hues
Rippled and swaying not-so-childhood memories
True visions in a false mirror
Abstract sky and I can hear its peacefulness
Curtains to my eyes

        —Alma Moxon, Grade 10

Poet/teacher Craig Czury, working with one of my classes, suggested a way of combining images in a poem about an important issue, to avoid using cliché or stereotyped ways of looking at a real concern. Write two clusters of images, the first beginning with something in your daily life that you are concerned about and the second with a global issue. Make sure that what you put in the cluster is a sensory image and not a general or abstract idea. Then combine images from the two clusters to write about the global concern.

War

The silent night of black and stars is wrenched apart
Bombers whistle like insects
Screams of yellow flame explode from a crumbling city lit
like a fairground for ...

Two middle-aged men who sign a paper with Cross pens
And lay down the tools as the journalists stand
The men in business suits grasp hands for ...

The rhythmic tramp-tramp of men carrying red banners whose
swastikas glare in the torchlight
Marching — left — expressionless — left — through — left —
right — left ...

A victory crowd in New York City, disturbing the hot summer
To wave to youths in sandy shirts
Dousing them with quick, bright confetti for ...

A cold damp body in a white shirt, no longer smelling the
grass and dirt
Smudged with clay
Wet with blood and tears
The fall from the eyes of a heap of grief weeping for ...

Maps and arrows and plans
Red lights on a switchboard
Soldiers in pick-ups grinning at ...

Rows of
White crosses
On a neatly cut
Field

Touched with
Glistening drops that
Obscure names under
The rain that gently, violently melts and fuses all
resistance and

Time passes

—Catharine Hornby, Grade 11

Ways of Seeing

Deposited upon the silent shore
Of memory, images and precious thoughts ...
—William Wordsworth

One reason for encouraging students to use images in their writing is to make them more observant of things in the world around them. A wonderful way of helping them see imaginatively is to have them write poems modeled on Wallace Stevens's "Thirteen Ways of Looking at a Blackbird."[14] This exercise helps students notice details, make connections, and understand the many different ways they react to an object or experience.

Poppy

A field of poppies
like a thousand vermillion butterflies
floating atop a swaying ocean of green.

A clandestine kiss
in the shadows
of a sweet, dark garden.
The poppy is the
unseen flush of her cheek.

The sunburned and freckled face
of a child
is the speckled heart of a poppy.

The foyer was empty and dusty,
and the tender, wilted petals of the
   poppy
were scattered
on the shimmering surface of the
   mahogany table.

The stroke of a blood-dipped brush
is the feathery petal of the poppy.

—Elizabeth Moxon, Grade 11

5 Ways of Looking at Darkness

Turning smiles to sadness,
the only lurking thing
was in the depths of darkness.

Dark shadows in the night
seeped into the woodwork
surrounded by darkness.

Silver green at nightfall
the lake sparkled
from darkness.

Darkness was the child's enemy
who soiled his dreams
and made him afraid.

At the sight of darkness,
things disappeared
Never to be seen again until dawn.

—Wiley Nelson, Grade 12

Ocean Waves

   I.   Following the lead of the dancing
        moon the ocean's waves.

  II.   Hungrily the ocean waves
        swallow the shore line.

 III.   Ocean waves enraged with fury
        slap the sand in violent beats.

 IV.   Ocean waves stung with salty
        infection.

  V.   Worn by the tides the ocean
        waves cradle the boat.

—Amy Hunter, Grade 12

The Objective Correlative

*Simonides calls painting silent poetry,
and poetry, silent painting.*

—Plutarch

With more advanced students, you might want to discuss T. S. Eliot's concept of the "objective correlative," which is an external equivalent for an emotion: objects, series of events, or situations that will evoke a specific emotion in the reader. Look for objective correlatives in poems the class is reading and writing. Even if you don't want to introduce the term, students of all ages can search for images that will let them express an emotion without naming it. When we were reading "The Seafarer," one of my tenth-grade classes looked for their own images of loneliness.[15]

I sat at my window watching the raindrops fall.
The tree grew into the shape of a Number One
in the midst of an empty field.
I tried to get in touch but could only hear the
      busy signal.
Then I sat still and listened to my heartbeat.

—Mai Abdala, Grade 10

Still

I see no ripples on the fishless lake
by the roofless wooden house
    where windows hide behind particle-board
    masks
I step onto the decaying porch, hoping
    the beams won't collapse,
    and I open a knobless front door.

Silence of cracking empty walls pays me no
    attention.
And now I know: grey, navy, black, olive, and one
    faded red-orange; cloth-bound books lie
    blanketed with age.
    none slips off when I lift the red one, even
    as I
    brush

Windows, thick at the top;
dead-gaze clocks,
empty, unyielding
    —unimpressionable—
mirrors,
and a lake that wouldn't ripple if I
    skipped a stone ...

                    —Liadan O'Callaghan, Grade 10

MUSIC: RHYTHM AND RHYME

[Poetry is] speech framed ... to be heard for its own sake and interest, even over and above the interest of meaning.

                    —Gerard Manley Hopkins

Many students like to write in a rigid pattern of rhythm and rhyme; they may believe that is what defines poetry. But very few middle and high school students can handle conventional rhythm and rhyme schemes well: When they try to fit a set pattern, they contort syntax and skew the meaning, usually trivializing a subject about which they have deep feelings. Early in the poetry writing, I begin to encourage my students to try writing in free verse. Usually, when two or three of them have written a poem in a conventional pattern and then rewrite the same idea in free verse, the class can see how much more genuine the free verse version sounds.

In some ways, free verse is more difficult than patterned poetry, because it requires writers to find the form that will express their thoughts best. For this very reason, free verse is usually a more effective means of expression for high school students and a better learning experience as well. Finding a form that fits the author's voice and the subject is equally necessary for prose writing and for poetry.

Free verse, although it has no set pattern to follow, does differ from prose significantly, and students can best learn what it is by reading and talking about good free verse poems. With a somewhat sophisticated group, you can do a careful analysis of some free verse to see how the internal elements structure the poem and hold it together. Whitman's "When Lilacs Last in the Dooryard Bloom'd" is a beautiful example of the movement in free verse through structure, language, and symbol.[16] "Corson's Inlet" by A. R. Ammons is another interesting example of a free verse poem that is carefully planned; it seems to move along very casually, rambling with the poet on his walk, but is actually carefully structured by elements within the poem.[17]

Try to shake students free from clinging to rigid forms in poetry writing at first. At some point, you may want to introduce them to the many patterns of rhythm and rhyme that are available. Imitating set forms can be fun, and it is sometimes very valuable because it gives students something secure to hold on to when they start writing. Concrete poetry, the diamanté, haiku, and tanka can help early writers learn important elements of poetry writing—in particular, concision, precise diction, and images. Later, when students have become more adept at using the language of poetry and the rhythms of free verse, and when they are comfortable with the idea that there is more to poetry than form, it is wonderful for them to experiment with forms that have prescribed rhythm and rhyme patterns, such as the ballad, limerick, sonnet, sestina, villanelle, or heroic couplet.

Rhythm

Of its own accord my song would come in the right rhythms, and what I was trying to say was poetry.

—Ovid

Poetry is to prose as dancing is to walking.

—John Wain

Poetry is rhythmical, even when it does not have a regular metrical beat. Free verse depends on rhythmic stresses and irregularities for its effect just as iambic pentameter blank verse does on its regular beat. Robert Bly recites his poetry to the strokes of a stringed instrument, much as ancient bards and scops did, to move the poetry, he says, from the head to the belly.

Rhythm is one of the subtlest and most difficult poetic concepts for student writers to understand. It can be first approached simply by finding lines in poetry that are rhythmically pleasing or effective or places where the rhythm doesn't seem to fit the subject and tone. Go lightly on this topic until your class has done quite a bit of poetry.

Rhyme

I rhyme for fun.

—Robert Burns

Rhyme is the rock on which thou art to wreck.

—John Dryden

Rhyme is simultaneously one of the delights and one of the problems of poetry writing. End rhymes, internal rhymes—the sound relationships of words are part of the intrinsic stuff of the poetic work. Yet a rigid adherence to rhyme schemes can be tyrannous and devastating for young writers, turning their poetry into formulaic mush. This thought is not new to modern free verse; as far back as the seventeenth century, John Milton talked about "the troublesome and modern bondage of rhyming," and said, "Rhyme [is] no necessary adjunct or true ornament of poem or good verse."[18] Ben Jonson wrote: "Greek was free from rhyme's infection/ Happy Greek, by this protection,/ Was not spoiled."[19] Of course, he wrote it in rhyme!

As poetry teacher, you need to be sensitive to both the pleasures and pains of rhyme. Confront the question of rhyme as soon as it comes up, and try at first to discourage dependence on regular masculine end rhymes, either as couplets or abcb rhymes—the two student favorites. Ask students who are just starting to write poetry to avoid end rhyme altogether for a while.

At the same time, emphasize the way poems always make use of internal rhymes—what Marianne Moore calls "not rhyme but echo." Find favorite poems with beautiful or striking internal rhyme and begin to sensitize students' ears to the interrelationships of sounds within a poem. Use the words *alliteration, assonance,* and *consonance* casually, and don't treat them as the arcane mysteries of an elite. (Demystify the elements of poetry at every opportunity!)

Reintroduce the concept of end rhyme only when students are comfortable with unrhymed poetry. Then look at both masculine rhyme and other forms of end rhyme; help students discover the effect of off-rhyme and the humor or softening of feminine rhymes. Point out again that end rhyme is not a necessary element of poetry.

LINE BREAKS

Prose is when all the lines except the last go on to the end.
Poetry is when some of them fall short of it.

—Jeremy Bentham

One decision a poet must make is where to end one poetic line and go on to the next. Line breaks are more important in writing poetry than most students realize, and this concept should be discussed fairly early in the poetry writing process. The word at the end of a line necessarily receives a special emphasis, not only visually but also in oral reading. When poetry rhymes, the impact of the last word is obvious, but it is also important in unrhymed verse. Usually, lines do not end with weak or unstressed words such as *the*. With the class, try some of the following exercises to help students understand the role of line breaks.

1. Read Gwendolyn Brooks's "We Real Cool," a poem that probably offers the most dramatic evidence you can muster to point out the importance of line breaks.[20] Give the class a copy of the poem in which you have moved *We* from the end of each line, where the poet placed it, to the beginning of the next line. Ask them to read aloud and see what this change does, not only to the meaning but also to the sound of the poem. (When Gwendolyn Brooks reads it, the final *We* is given a tremendous emphasis and a rather long pause before the next line.) Then examine other poems that have unusual line breaks. Many of e. e. cummings's poems provide interesting examples of unconventional breaks, as do William Carlos Williams's "The Red Wheelbarrow," "This Is Just to Say," and "The Ivy Crown."[21]

2. Have students take a poem of their own and play with changing the line breaks. Ask them to write the poem out in three or four different ways and then consider what each variation does in terms of meaning and sound, as well as how it looks on the page. Try moving lines to different positions on the page, not all aligned at the left margin. Exchange experiments with other members of the writing group or with a partner; discuss which way they prefer. Which "feels" better when it's read aloud and when it's read silently?

3. At various points during the year, bring up the concept of line breaks in connection both with students' writing and with poetry they read in class. Occasionally have students look through their folders specifically to examine poems for line breaks. Let them see some of your own poems and discuss with them your decisions on line breaks.

4. Ask students to experiment with writing prose poems, which look like prose but read like poetry. Carrying an idea from one line to the next without breaking it or punctuating it sometimes helps their poetry sound more natural.

Me

I am a letter in a newspaper, a robot in a factory. I am
an eagle that flies high in the sky, then an anchor that sinks
to the bottom of the ocean. I exist as a flower in a field of
weeds only to be picked by a little girl. I am the roll of the
dice, a zipper, or a seventeen magazine. I am a warm wool
sweater or a pair of sunglasses that reflect the sun. I'm a
used sweatshirt one depends on to keep warm, sleep after a
tiring day or weeping after a death in the family. I'm the
somebody everybody knows, but can't remember their
name. I exist in the minds of the oppressed. I'm the picture
on the wall that stirs you to tears, I'm the difference
between night and day, black and white, and good and
evil. I'm the girl that never existed.

— Jennifer Jones, Grade 10

Falling

Then the leaf was whirling, whizzing through the wind. It was carried like a paper toy, with neither speed nor direction. It had traveled far from home; the high maple, grand and golden, loomed above it. Finally the wisp of color reached its destination, dropped to the ground and fell like a feather among other leaves. And just as this one had, others rambled down, rustling the earth as they escaped their hold. Soon a pile had gathered, all burning with their colors, surely to be joined by others.

—Caroline Dawson, Grade 10

STANZAIC FORM

A dance is a measured pace, as a
verse is a measured speech.

—Francis Bacon

The stanza is the basic structural unit in poetry, a group of lines separated from other lines by a space. In traditional poetry, stanzas are usually arranged in definite patterns, but in more recent work, writers use a wider variety of stanza forms and lengths. The choice of stanza form is an important decision for poets. Will they write in free verse or in one of the many formulaic patterns, such as rhymed couplet, haiku, sonnet, or blank verse?

In free verse, stanza breaks, like line breaks, are left to the poet's discretion, and they affect the meaning of a poem, its appearance, and its sound. Breaks between stanzas also indicate a pause when the poem is read. Stanzas do not always need to end with a period, nor must they start at the beginning of a sentence. Some contemporary free verse poets divide their work into repeated patterns—tercets (three-line stanzas), quatrains (four-line), and so on. Others are totally free, with varied stanza lengths or no stanza breaks at all. Punctuation is optional. Introduce your students to the possibilities open to them in both patterned and free verse, and encourage them to experiment with this aspect of form.

1. Copy a free verse poem without stanza breaks and ask the class to play with dividing it in several different ways, discussing the effect of different breaks. You might give the same poem to all writing groups to break apart and then have them compare their preferences. Then look at the original poem to see the author's own stanza breaks. Discuss the implications.

2. Have students each take a poem from their folders and experiment with different stanza breaks. Try dividing the poem into two-line units, three lines, or four; try irregular breaks or no breaks. Decide which form best expresses the idea. Showing various versions of poems on the overhead projector facilitates discussion of the concept of stanza breaks.

3. When your class has become experienced and competent with free verse, have students imitate some defined stanza forms, such as ballad stanza, limerick, or sonnet. Discuss the relationship between stanza form and meaning: Are there topics or moods that might be best expressed by being confined in a set pattern, and others better in free verse?

STANZA ORDER

There is a music wherever there is a
harmony, order or proportion.

—Robert Browning

Sometimes a poem can be improved by changing the order of the stanzas; rearrangement should always be an option for reworking or revising a poem. It's not unusual for a writer to give too much information at the beginning of a poem or to go on too long at the end in an attempt to "wrap up" or spell out a conclusion that the reader has already reached. The most compelling stanza may be buried somewhere in the middle of the poem and need to be placed in a better position. The following activities provide some ways students may work with the idea of changing stanza order, or cutting, for more powerful poetry.

1. Give the class someone else's poem to work with as an experiment in rearranging stanzas. One of your own poems would be a generous offer, because students sometimes are reluctant to tamper with an author's printed work in such a radical way. Using a poem of yours once again provides an opportunity for students to discuss a writer's decisions with that writer. Wallace Stevens's own suggested rearrangement of stanzas in his poem "Sunday Morning" also makes a very interesting basis for discussion.[22] Why did Stevens change his mind about the stanza order after the poem was published?

2. Ask students to experiment with stanza order in their own poems.

   • Actually cut a poem apart with scissors and rearrange it in various ways.

   • On the word processor, rearrange stanzas several ways and compare the results.

   • Find the most interesting line of the poem and begin with that line, rearranging the stanzas to follow.

   • Try putting the opening stanza at the end.

   • Try putting the ending stanza somewhere else in the poem.

   • Try cutting out the ending.

   • Try cutting out the opening.

These exercises are more fun if they are done with the writing group or a partner.

BEGINNINGS AND ENDINGS

Great is the art of beginning, but greater the art of
ending; many a poem is marred by a superfluous
verse.

— Henry Wadsworth Longfellow

All writers want the opening of a piece of writing to engage the reader, arouse curiosity and interest in the writing, and draw the reader into the experience or idea. One of the most typical problems of student writers is to say too much at the beginning and not to leave enough to the reader's imagination. Groups should always discuss the effectiveness of a poem's opening.

The ending of a poem, like the ending of any piece of writing, is also an element for particular scrutiny. A common tendency in poetry writing, and in prose as well, is to try to sum up or wrap up everything that has been said or to draw a moral. It is worth spending a little time to look at the endings of several very good free verse poems and determine what contemporary authors try to do with endings. Writing groups should consider the question of beginnings and endings when they discuss each other's poems. Experiment with both elements.

1. Take a poem from the folder and try removing parts of the opening — a word, a single line, several lines, the whole opening stanza.

2. Take a poem and fold over the last line, the last few lines, or the last stanza. Is the ending needed? Ask the writing group to suggest where the poem might end.

3. Take the ending and put it at the beginning. Or take the beginning and put it at the end. Do either of those changes (with or without any additional revision) improve the poem?

4. Ask the writing group to choose what they think is the most interesting line of the poem. Would that line work as an opening or as an ending?

REPETITION

Play it again, Sam.

— Misquotation from
Casablanca

Repetition is a very effective poetic device when it is deliberate and not a result of unthinking verbosity or laziness in looking for new words. Help the class understand repetition with the following exercises.

1. Look at some poems that use repetition in a way you find interesting. Some good poets, widely anthologized, are Walt Whitman (from almost any section of *Song of Myself*),[23] Gwendolyn Brooks ("We Real Cool"),[24] Sylvia Plath ("Lady Lazarus," "Daddy," "Death & Co."),[25]

and William Butler Yeats ("Three Things," "Mad as the Mist and Snow," "Those Dancing Days Are Gone").[26] Discuss the poet's use of repetition. What does repetition do for each poem?

2. Choose a poetic line that appeals to you because of its meaning, sound, or imagery (it may be a line from one of your earlier poems, a newly written line, or even a quotation from another poem), and write a poem in which the line is repeated in one of the following ways:

- as the beginning of each stanza

Waiting for You

I'm sitting here waiting for your call,
The chimes of the grandfather clock tick slowly by,
Music fills the depressed atmosphere
The sun sinks lower in the sky.

I'm sitting here waiting for your voice,
To call my name out and be heard by all,
Your voice can draw me in,
Pull me closer to your heart.

I'm sitting here waiting for your touch,
Your gentle fingertips on my skin,
Like a lullaby that puts me to sleep,
So your touch puts me at ease.

I'm sitting here waiting for your love,
How long will it take for you to love me again?
To miss you, to need you, to want you,
Is all I can sit here and wait for.

— Alma Moxon, Grade 10

- as the ending of each stanza

- as the first and last lines of the poem

- within stanzas

- in some pattern of your own devising

- at random

3. Repeat a pattern within a poem. For example, begin lines with the same word or phrase.

I Inherited

I inherited my eyes from my father and
    kiss from my mother
I inherited the mind of both
I inherited love from my Creator and
    hate from the unknown
I inherited softness from the morning
    and hardness from the night
I might have known of inherited
    trouble—

I inherited my song from the
    hummingbird and shrill from
    the mermaid
I inherited my touch from Midas and
    my laugh from the queen of ages
I inherited ... I am UnIqUe—

—Merina Wijaya, Grade 11

4. Experiment with unstructured repetition.

Winter

She was beautiful
whether she believed me or not
her hair
was beautiful

Watched her enter the
white
room with
ice stares
watched her watch the
ice stares
bounce off her deep red
dress, her
deep
red
soul.

Watched her hold the
deep
red
wine in her
cold
hand over the
white
rug.

Watched her fight away
cold
deep
grins, trying to obey her own self

Watched her press her
cold
legs lightly together and lick her
deep
red
lipstick off her lips.

Watched her fight away any
temptation to get involved
Watched her
kill
long
ice
stares that bounced right off her

Watched her wonder
watched her wish
watched her cling
watched her promises to herself
melt
away
watched her wash away
red
blood
remarks
watched her run away from
feelings, thoughts
of ever being
beautiful.

She was beautiful.
Her hair,
her heart,
her soul.

Her soul was
beautiful.

—Christina Jimenez, Grade 10

5. For very sophisticated students, the patterned repetition demanded by the sestina or villanelle is challenging. (See the villanelles "One Art" by Elizabeth Bishop[27] and "Do Not Go Gentle into That Good Night" by Dylan Thomas[28] or the sestina "Remembering Kevan MacKenzie" by Henry Taylor[29] for examples of the forms.)

TONE

Sphere-born harmonious sisters,
Voice and Verse.

—John Milton

Tone may be defined as the tone of voice of the speaker, or the speaker's attitude toward the subject. Tone does not just "color" a poem; it is an integral part of the meaning. Student writers need to become aware of the importance of tone, although it can be a difficult concept to teach. The best approach to help students understand tone is simply to point out, first in literature and then in their own poetry, ways in which diction, figurative language, and images work to convey the speaker's attitude.

1. In class: Look at several poems that have a powerful and unmistakable tone, such as Sylvia Plath's "Daddy";[30] Gwendolyn Brooks's "We Real Cool";[31] e. e. cummings's "Buffalo Bill's Defunct," Emily Dickinson's "Apparently with no surprise" (J. 1624);[32] or Robert Browning's "Soliloquy of the Spanish Cloister" or "My Last Duchess."[33] Discuss the way wording, rhythmic patterns, rhyme, images, and metaphors create the tone in each poem.

2. How does the author's tone lead you to interpret the subject of a poem? Look at several poems written on the same topic (for example, death or war) and discuss the different attitudes that are projected by the poets' tone.

3. Take one poem from your folder. Have someone else read the poem aloud to the writing group and ask the group to define its tone. Does the group hear the tone the writer intended? Is the tone clear and consistent? Should it be strengthened or clarified anywhere? If the tone changes during the course of the poem, was it meant to? Does the change contribute to the meaning?

TITLES

To call a thing by name is to make it so.

—Ralph Ellison

Even though many students will resist titling to the bitter end, I try to persuade them that every poem should be given a title. Being forced to title a poem makes the poet question its essence and what is most important in it. Often someone else in the writing group or class can help the poet find a title. Sometimes other people's suggestions are so far off it helps the poet see what the real title is! As a last resort, the first line or phrase of the poem may be used.

Have students look at all the poems in their folders with the writing group or a partner and examine the titles. Are there any that could be improved? Which ones are both appropriate and interesting?

REVISING

And perhaps the writer's greatest freedom, as artist, lies precisely in his possession of technique; for it is through technique that he comes to possess and express the meaning of life.

—Ralph Ellison

A writer is unfair to himself when he is unable to be hard on himself.

—Marianne Moore

Ralph Ellison's statement points out what may be the most profound reason for students to struggle with sharpening their writing technique.[34] Working with an idea, a feeling, a memory, a vision, trying to express it in the most precise and interesting way, leads to clarification, insight, and meaning *for the writer*. In this section I offer some very specific suggestions for helping a class understand why and how to work on technique through revision.

Students should know that most poets do revise and rework their poetry—of course, some more than others. James Merrill says that the first draft of a poem is in anyone's words; it becomes your own only in rewriting and revising. Stephen Spender, in his essay "The Making of a Poem," describes the process of writing a single poem; after his first attempts, he says, "In the next *twenty versions* of the poem I *felt my way towards* the clarification of the seen picture, the music and the inner feeling"[35] (italics mine). Other poets write more quickly and do less radical revision, and for every writer some poems need more work than others.

Make revising a regular part of class during the writing workshop period.

1. Begin by showing the class what revising means; suggest various ways to approach it. Ask for volunteers to put their poems on an overhead projector transparency. With the whole class, look at the poems and make suggestions for revision.

2. Model revision techniques by working on your own poems on the overhead projector: Explain your choices, note places where you are dissatisfied, and ask for students' help.

3. Try to organize the writing period so that there is time in class after groups meet for students to start working on revisions.

4. Sometimes devote a larger part of the period to revising by asking students each to take a poem from the folder and look at it in specific ways. (See the suggestions below.)

5. Make a radical revision, such as a point of view change, a new exercise for an old poem by each student.

6. Now and then make revision the assignment instead of new writing.

7. Use revision occasionally as a group rather than an individual activity: Have writing groups work together on a revision exercise.

As always in teaching writing, you should be very specific when you assign an exercise. Help students understand various methods of working on technique by asking them to revise in some of the following ways.

Look again at the original vision or impetus for the poem.

1. Individually, or with the group, identify one part of the poem (a stanza, image, or idea) that is particularly striking. Freewrite associations around that part. Does the freewriting bring up more detail that would improve the poem? Does it make you want to add to the poem or take anything out? Does it change the focus or direction of the poem? Does it make you want to write a different poem?

2. Take one key word and create a "cluster" to elicit more detail or perhaps to change the direction of the poem, or to evoke a new poem.

3. Do the same with "looping."

4. Consider expansion. Do any parts of the poem need more detail or explanation?

5. Discuss clarification. Should any parts be clearer or more understandable than they are? (Always remember that logical sense may not be the poet's main objective!)

6. Change the point of view from which the poem was written.

    *   If it is in first person (the "I" narrator), change it to third person ("he/she").

    *   Rewrite the experience from another person's point of view, making the narrator someone else within the poem, or totally outside it, observing impartially.

- Change *I* to *you* and see how that affects the feeling or tone.

- Rewrite the poem as a persona poem, taking on the "I" voice for someone who is not you.

Look at structure and consistency.

1. Find the best line in the poem and make it the first line of a new poem.

2. Look at transitions from one part of the poem to the next. Are they unnecessarily confusing or unnecessarily explicit?

3. Try breaking a poem into numbered sections without transitions. Try putting together some different poems on the same topic with numbered sections.

4. Follow suggestions given in this chapter for working on line breaks, stanza breaks, or stanza order.

5. Look for variation in sentence structure: Consider whether there should be variation and whether parallelism or change make the poem more striking or less interesting.

6. Try rewriting a poem with and without a rhythm or rhyme pattern.

7. Check for consistency of metaphor. If metaphors change within the poem, is there a deliberate reason, or are they accidentally mixed metaphors? Does this add or detract?

8. Check for consistency of tone. Whose voice do you hear? Does the voice or attitude change? If so, is that change deliberate?

Look at language.

1. Look at verbs. How strong are the verbs? How many times do you use a form of the verb *to be*? Would some other verbs give a more active feeling to the poem or a stronger picture?

2. Look at verb tenses. Would this poem be better if it were written in past, present, or a perfect tense?

3. Look at nouns. Have you used interesting, strong, varied nouns?

4. Look at all the adverbs. Are they really necessary? Adverbs often weaken a poem. Could you find a verb that would include the meaning of the adverb?

5. Look at adjectives. Are they all necessary and interesting? What do they add to the images?

6. Look at any word or phrase you think may be overworked or cliché and try to find a new way to express the idea or image. Is the idea or image itself overworked?

7. Look for unnecessary words. What could be cut out without changing anything significant? Where would cutting make the poem stronger?

8. Look for "purple passages," with overwritten and overdone language. Simplify such passages.

9. Look for unnecessary repetition (remembering that repetition is often an effective poetic device). Have you repeated when you didn't need to or even mean to?

10. Look for redundancy. Have you used several words that really mean the same thing? Is an idea unnecessarily restated in the same or different terms?

11. Check for consistency and appropriateness of diction.

12. Follow the suggestions in this chapter for looking at poetic language, strong words, figurative language, or diction.

13. Look at punctuation and capitalization of words. Are all of the choices deliberate? Do both punctuation and capitalization serve the purpose of the poem well?

Leaving a poem alone for a while and then coming back to it some time later often gives the writer fresh eyes with which to look at it. Plan deliberate "time lapses" to give students some space between the writing and revising stages.

The writing group can provide both an incentive and a support for revision and should always be ready to make suggestions for places or ways to revise. Remind groups again to operate by the "P's and Q's": Praise first, then Question. The poet, of course, always has the last say about a poem and may or may not decide to take the group's — or the teacher's — advice. Be sure students know that final choices are always the author's.

Remember too that a poem can be over-revised. Student writers, especially those new to poetry writing, sometimes want to back off from their most surprising and interesting moments in favor of a more conventional way of saying something; overworking can lead them to revert to stilted phrases and common images. One way to ward off this tendency is by repeatedly pointing out and praising the freshest and most striking bits of their writing to the class. Students should always keep their drafts and revisions for comparison; then they can go back to an earlier version if they or the group decide it was better.

To show students that published poets, too, consider revision important, give the class an opportunity to look at and discuss some choices other authors have made for changing poems. A particularly interesting comparison may be made between the two versions of D. H. Lawrence's poem about his mother, the notebook draft "The Piano" and the revised poem "Piano," in which Lawrence cut out two stanzas and compressed his ideas in interesting ways.[36] You can also find radically altered versions of poems by William Butler Yeats,[37] and reproduced manuscripts of some of Emily Dickinson's poems show the care and precision of her choice in words.[38] Look at the different versions of the poems and discuss the choices: Why were the changes made? What decisions about vision, focus, structure, and language was the author making by the changes? You can add depth by bringing in some of the revisions you have made on a poem of your own for the class to discuss: In this case, the author is present to explain the decision to change, cut, or expand. Some students will also be eager to share their own revision choices with the class.

WRITER'S BLOCK

A man may write at any time, if he will
set himself doggedly to it.

—Samuel Johnson

At some point during the year, you might have students who complain that they can't write because of "writer's block." Sometimes students do genuinely hit a dry period when poetry writing becomes almost impossible. Sometimes they just think they have hit such a period, either because of reluctance (even fear) of continuing or because it feels dramatic to have writer's block. When either situation occurs, it's useful to have some ideas you can give students to start the flow of writing going again. Here are several things you can suggest that students try.

1. Write the assignment in prose.

2. Do one or more freewritings about the assignment or the topic you would like to write about.

3. Do one or more clusters centered on the topic or on an entirely different concept.

4. Write a poem about writer's block.

5. Write a prose description of writer's block.

6. Write a notebook entry about this particular writer's block: Try to describe and analyze it.

7. Write a prose poem letter to a poet whose work you admire.

8. Write a letter to yourself to read a year from now (seal the letter and put it away in a dresser drawer with the date it's to be opened written on the front).

9. Do a notebook entry from the list "Fictionalizing" or "Exaggerating Reality" (chapter 3). Turn it into a poem.

10. Take a notebook entry you have done from the "Figurative Language" list (chapter 3) and write a nonsense poem using some of the figures. Or combine several entries.

11. Write a collaborative poem with a friend. Write the whole thing together or write alternate lines.

12. Write a collaborative poem with your writing group.

13. Write a group poem that starts with a line from a poem you like. Add a line of your own, then fold over the paper, letting only your line show, and pass it on. Each person adds a line and keeps folding the paper so any writer sees only the last line that was written.

14. Write a nonsense poem with your writing group or with a friend.

15. Do a "mistranslation" of a poem from a language you don't know.

16. Using some other translations as resources, translate a poem from a language you do know.

17. Read some poems other students have written. Look through old literary magazines, national magazines of student writing, class collections, and so on.

18. Read published poetry. Especially, read a number of poems by the same author.

19. Read some good prose.

20. Go away from writing and do something else for a while, letting your ideas percolate by themselves. Talk with a friend, read, go outdoors, bake brownies.

21. Do some vigorous physical exercise. Activities such as swimming, walking, running, or even mowing the lawn often get a rhythm flowing, and when the body is doing repetitive exercise the mind is freed to float imaginatively.

NOTES

[1]Kenneth Koch. Class at Columbia University, 1988.

[2]Shakespearean sonnets and poems by John Donne, Percy Bysshe Shelley, or John Keats may be found in Helen McDonnell, John Pfordresher, and Gladys V. Veidemanis, eds. *England in Literature.* Glenview, IL: Scott, Foresman, 1987.

[3]Poems by Emily Dickinson, Walt Whitman, Allen Ginsburg, or Sylvia Plath may be found in George Perkins, Scully Bradley, Richmond C. Beatty, and E. Hudson Long, eds. *The American Tradition in Literature*. New York: Random House, 1985.

[4]Emily Dickinson. *The Manuscript Books of Emily Dickinson*. Cambridge, MA: Belknap Press of Harvard University Press, 1981.

[5]"To His Excellency George Washington" by Phillis Wheatley may be found in Hilary Russell, ed. *The Longman Anthology of American Poetry*. New York: Longman, 1992.

[6]"The Leap" by James Dickey may be found in Russell.

[7]Poems by Emily Dickinson may be found in Perkins, Bradley, Beatty, and Long.

[8]Poems by Walt Whitman may be found in ibid.

[9]Poems by Emily Dickinson may be found in ibid.

[10]Poems by Robert Bly may be found in ibid.

[11]Poems by Elizabeth Bishop may be found in Russell.

[12]Poems by A. R. Ammons, Adrienne Rich, and William Carlos Williams may be found in Perkins, Bradley, Beatty, and Long.

[13]Poems by Walt Whitman may be found in ibid.

[14]Wallace Stevens's "Thirteen Ways of Looking at a Blackbird" may be found in Kenneth Koch and Kate Farrell. *Sleeping on the Wing*. New York: Vintage Books, 1982.

[15]"The Seafarer" may be found in McDonnell, Pfordresher, and Veidemanis.

[16]Poems by Walt Whitman may be found in Perkins, Bradley, Beatty, and Long.

[17]Poems by A. R. Ammons may be found in ibid.

[18]John Milton's preface to *Paradise Lost* may be found in *The Complete Poetry of John Milton*. New York: Doubleday, 1971, 249.

[19]Ben Jonson's *A Fit of Rime Against Rime* may be found in H. R. Woudhuysen, ed. *The Penguin Book of Renaissance Verse*. London: Penguin Press, 1992, 718.

[20]Gwendolyn Brooks's "We Real Cool" may be found in X. J. Kennedy, ed. *An Introduction to Poetry*. Boston: Little, Brown, 1971.

[21]Poems by William Carlos Williams may be found in Perkins, Bradley, Beatty, and Long.

[22]Wallace Stevens's "Sunday Morning" (including a footnote about the author's stanza order suggestions) may be found in ibid.

[23]Poems by Walt Whitman may be found in ibid.

[24]Poems by Gwendolyn Brooks may be found in Kennedy.

[25]Poems by Sylvia Plath may be found in Perkins, Bradley, Beatty, and Long.

[26]Poems by William Butler Yeats may be found in *The Collected Poems of William Butler Yeats*. New York: Macmillan, 1956.

[27]Elizabeth Bishop's "One Art" may be found in Russell.

[28]Dylan Thomas's "Do Not Go Gentle into That Good Night" may be found in McDonnell, Pfordresher, and Veidemanis.

[29]Henry Taylor's "Remembering Kevan MacKenzie" may be found in Kennedy.

[30]Sylvia Plath's "Daddy" may be found in Perkins, Bradley, Beatty, and Long.

[31]Gwendolyn Brooks's "We Real Cool" may be found in Kennedy.

[32]e. e. cummings's "Buffalo Bill's Defunct" and Emily Dickinson's "Apparently with no surprise" (J. 1624) may be found in Perkins, Bradley, Beatty, and Long.

[33]Poems by Robert Browning may be found in McDonnell, Pfordresher, and Veidemanis.

[34]Ralph Ellison. *Shadow and Act*. New York: Vintage Books, 1953, 163.

[35]Stephen Spender. "The Making of a Poem." In *The Creative Process: A Symposium*, ed. Ghiselin Brewster. New York and Scarborough, ON: New American Library, 1952, 117.

[36]The two versions of D. H. Lawrence's poem appear in McDonnell, Pfordresher, and Veidemanis.

[37]A splendid source of early drafts of William Butler Yeats's work is Curtis B. Bradford. *Yeats at Work*. Carbondale and Edwardsville: Southern Illinois University Press, 1965. Part I, pages 3-168, contains various draft versions of the poems. Parts II and III contain drafts of the plays and prose. Two illustrations of Yeats's changes from draft to finished poem appear in Richard Ellman. *Yeats: The Man and the Masks*. New York: W. W. Norton, 1979, 145-147, 174-175. Yeats's various changes in the poems from early to late publication appear in Peter Allt and Russell K. Alspach. *The Variorum Edition of the Poems of W. B. Yeats*. New York: Macmillan, 1968.

[38]Emily Dickinson. *The Manuscript Books of Emily Dickinson*. Cambridge, MA: Belknap Press of Harvard University Press, 1981.

6 Creating Poetry Writing Topics

*Poetry is simply the most beautiful way of
saying something, and hence its importance.*
— Matthew Arnold

All students have a store of imaginative energy just waiting to be released. By giving them interesting ideas for writing, we can spark that energy into creativity. A good topic not only inspires the flash that starts students writing, but also helps them write in imaginative ways. Simply saying, "Write a poem!" is likely to ignite panic rather than poetry; finding good writing topics for your particular class may be the most important thing you do as a poetry teacher.

Poetry can rise from an event, an idea, an image, an observation, an emotion, language, weird combinations of words or associations, a desire to communicate, or a desire to unload a feeling—sometimes from a mysterious unknown place in the poet. Topics can also originate in a subject the class is studying, an idea that comes up in class, a poem someone in the class writes, or something they read. Students themselves often come up with interesting themes for the class to write about. Be on the lookout for sources of poetic assignments in the world we inhabit, in students' own interests, and in other poetry the literature class reads.

FINDING TOPICS IN THE
WORLD AROUND YOU

*Life comes before literature, as the material
always comes before the work. The hills are full
of marble before the world blooms with statues.*
— Phillips Brooks

Ideas for poetry writing abound in the world of the observer. In this section, I offer a number of lists of topics I have used recently, with examples of the poems my students wrote in response. I start with more (apparently) impersonal topics because they seem safer to many beginners. These lists are by no means exhaustive. You'll find that, once you begin looking for them, ideas for poetry come from almost anywhere.

Poems That Start in Language

1. Make ugly and beautiful word lists, play poetry poker, or do some mistranslation (see chapter 4).

2. From a number of words written on separate pieces of paper on the bulletin board, pick one and write a poem that uses that word.

Cherries

> smooth, plump
> pert red explosions
> satin
> to touch
> —split in half
> to reveal
> the tender, crimson
> protection
> of a stone heart.

> —Jane Lee-You, Grade 12
> (starting from the word *pert*)

3. From a poem that is read aloud, list appealing words or phrases on the board and then write a poem using many of them.

4. List interesting words or phrases from the writer's notebooks, and write a poem using many of them.

> my body lies
>   deep
> in the dead forest
> my eyes cannot catch
> the hard sun
> the shivering grind
> of vampyric mosquitoes
> echoes in my ears
> i am trying to unbury
> myself,
> but somehow,
> someone
> keeps throwing dirt
> in my face

> —Sian Killingsworth,
>   Grade 12

5. From a list of eight or ten words—drawn from poetry poker cards, a published poem, or the teacher or class's imagination—write a poem that contains all the words.

6. Write a poem composed of lines from songs.

> I want to be wild again,
> Don't care what they say,
> Lost in the shadows,
> People are strange.
> Let the good times roll,
> Stand by me, I feel free,
> Destination unknown, Playing
> With the boys
> Living in a five o'clock world
> All I have to do is dream, send
> me an angel,
> Don't let the sun go down on me,
> I still believe, what a wonderful world.
>
> —Kim Gentempo, Grade 10

7. Write a poem that just plays with the sounds of words.

Imp

> Terra cotta flip.
> Shrimp prim primrose.
> In on coconut in butter on cocoa.
> Sofa brook? Sofa brook.
> Jar, jarring, jarred, ajar, a jar.
> The terrace says—
> Rag you? Rag you. Rag you!
>
> The terrace says rugby yells yes.
> Grim up globe vex grim.
> Rugby yells yes.
> slur ... slur ... slur; smoothly slur.
> A winter agog jolts jerk jog.
> Soup is mutual!
>
> —Carin Companick, Grade 11

8. Take a quotation you like and write a poem with the quotation as an epigraph.

9. Start with figures of speech, such as metaphor, simile, personification, hyperbole, or apostrophe.

The Tree

> A beautiful ballet dancer
> thin, delicate fingers
> reaching the sky.
> Body arched
> swaying in time to the
> rhythmic wind.
>
> —Jennie Park, Grade 11

> a new word trickles,
> drips from the pen,
> landing softly on the pillow
> paper ...
>
> —Justine Schiro, Grade 11

10. Write a poem that contains an extended metaphor or simile.

Apologies

I'm saying sorry
even though I believe I did nothing wrong,
Saying sorry might make you feel guilty,
because you know that it wasn't my fault either,
But now I'm saying sorry to see what your reaction is —
whether you will stop, sigh, and look at me,
or continue to build your wall of neglect,
Brick after brick you close yourself away,
and soon you won't see the sunlight,
I suppose you'll want to say sorry too —
apology not accepted,
And I begin to build my wall,
Ten bricks and the wall reaches my knees,
Now I can't walk towards you — back to you,
Twenty bricks and the wall reaches my waist,
Now you can't hold me,
Forty bricks and the fortress is up to my neck,
My arms can't reach out to touch you,
I think I won't put my eyes behind the wall,
I want to see you sit behind your wall,
And I want to hear you —
Hear you say "I'm sorry,"
Holding your image in my mind

—Shelley Wollert, Grade 10

Woman

Rooted resolutely
Lone green stalk stands straight
Whorled sepals crown the slender strand.
Calyx cups the flaming crimson blossom
Striking to those who cast a glance
Each vibrant petal passion's purest form.
Yet to those who look within
A haven to bees and beetles alike.
A creator of life
Essence of redness
Essential to nature's cycle
Woman.

—Holly Light, Grade 11

11. Use parts of speech in new ways.

Three O'Clock

I've merry-go-rounded the kitchen
On the blade of the ceiling fan
At medium speed

And know well the faces of each
White polka-dot on the back of
A faded navy blue cobbler's apron

My elbows stick to humidity
Tableclothing the table
The fan in the window
Hallucinates

There is nothing left to draw.

—Carin Companick, Grade 11

12. Start with some very odd or quirky association someone else gives you. (For example, in a workshop I attended recently, participants were given the topic "How is your father like the back of your hand, and how is your father like the palm of your hand?")

Poems That Start in Form

1. Write a concrete poem (a poem that takes the physical shape of its subject).

2. If you are not "haiku'd out," write haiku or tanka to create compelling images.

A clear stream trinkles
I have a closer look
My reflection is missing.

—Kathryn Calogredes,
Grade 10

3. Write a series of haiku or short haiku-like poems on the same subject.

He

Crossed in
And leaving a trace,
Steve is black.

At the sight of beauty,
Why do you lust over it?
A man *is* a man.

The wind is swift
And the breeze cool.
Warm air remembers—
Jamaica.

Within a world
Of millions
The smoothness of Steve's
Skin is all I know.

The ball fell
And night is among us.
The new day begins
And Steve is resting.

—Najah Mas'udi, Grade 11

4. Write a diamanté.

5. Write a ballad, imitating the form of the ballad stanza.

O Daughter

"Oh where have you been, my daughter?
And why are you out so late?
You know you are to be home at midnight!"
  "I was out with my boyfriend, mother,
  I am tired, may I go to bed?"

"You didn't answer my question,
Where have you been, my daughter?
I've been worried, I thought
Something might have happened to you."
  "I am fine, mother, I was out
  with my boyfriend. Please, mother,
  I am tired, may I go to bed?" (etc.)

—Danielle Vaughan, Grade 10

6. Write a narrative poem.

7. Experiment with punctuation, capitalization, and other mechanical devices.

Scattered, Displaced

i WANT to JUMP in the world of PLAY
i WANT to DANCE with the dog and the wind
my bright green CLASHING with a crisp brown
all RACING to the finish line
a jungle gym GONE CRAZY at night
where only the fox and cat CAN CRAWL
and children ARE so HAPPY
and they ARE JOKING around
ISN'T it fun to FOOL the moon?
it DOES not always COME out
and PLAY your broken guitar
that SITS under the lamplight
it IS all MIXED up and SCATTERED, DISPLACED
GONE almost WILD
i EXPECT exactly what i SEE.

—Christina Jimenez, Grade 10

8. Write a poem that is all a single sentence.

Tiles of Childhood

The tiles of when
I sat on my dad's glasses
and wept on the floor
as I stared at his blank expression
and that scooter like a giraffe
with the red wheels
that never went in the right direction
that my brother never let me ride
by the pool
the pool where I wore the orange bubble
and watched the others
dive into the deep end
and my dad gave me hotdogs
on the white Pitmann-Moore plates
and my mom spelled my name in ketchup
she wore the terry cloth dress
and her shoulders were burnt in the seventies
and my brother had his imaginary friend George
who i never met
but Mark let me ride the lawnmower with him
up and down the lawns
between the trees
the trees where we sat
and my mom took our Christmas card photo
and i never wanted to go near the tree
with the snake pit
and the flowers out front were effortless
and I don't remember ever watering them
I once dove in the mud
just to see what it felt like
and I wanted so badly
to run out on the pool cover

—Shelley Wollert, Grade 10

9. Write a prose poem.

Spring in the Blue Ridge

drinking Hawaiian Punch from a soda can on
Skyline Drive I was listening to the Beach
Boys on my walkman I was scared

we were going to drive off a cliff like that stone
wall all crumbled to pieces everyone joking
about cars that didn't make it around the
sharp corner teasing me my brother gets out
at a view point and crouches on the other side
of the wall trying to make me think he's fallen
off the cliff and hanging onto the wall but I
got out and the high altitude made me feel
giddy and light-headed

and then Skyland Lodge on one of the highest
peaks the balconies out over the edge of the
cliff it was so beautiful and spectacular I
wasn't scared anymore I felt like I was high or
drunk or something the air was doing it to me
this place was so amazing

as we're driving slowly and I've got my head out
the window taking in the cool pure spring air
the mist hanging between the mountains
looked like white rivers the dogwoods buds
birds butterflies deer I felt so carefree like I'm
going to live forever (Hawaiian Punch must
make me drunk) but everything is so perfect
and still

I want to go back
                                    —Laura Fitton, Grade 10

10. Make a poem that is an abstraction from a longer poem.

11. Imitate poetry for children (nursery rhymes or poems by Dr. Seuss or
    Shel Silverstein, for example) and read your poem to a child.

Poems That Start in the Life of the Writer

1. Describe a special place in your life, present or past.

Sea Girt

Distant rattling train tracks, salty ocean air,
sandy sandwiches, the forbidden leather chair,
the hum of the air conditioner and splinters on the boardwalk,
the irritating, wonderful smell of moth balls, the familiar
    cracked sidewalk
Sea glass whale, body surfing, cheese and crackers, bicycle
    exploration,
monkey bars and iron horses, police slash fire station.
Ice cream on the car floor, maple seeds on your nose.
Shell garden, my little red car, and picture windows,
Barbie's at Bushy's, twin beds, and Circle Freeze,
Fold-out dining table, fireflies, and holly trees,
ashes on the right, yellow carpet, poker for candy,
Pop-Pop's veggies, snake-oriental rug, Bloody Mary,
game shows, tiger ashtray, Foodtown, and lighthouse,
needlepoint, red toenail polish, and boy and girl mouse,
Brown shell wallpaper, Peddler's Village, and playing cards,
flattened pennies on the railroad, funny glass jars ...

From the distant rattling train tracks follows a wave
of endless memories.

—Meaghan Mountford, Grade 12

2. Describe a refuge, a place of safety.

3. Write a poem responding to something somebody said to you.

You, Young Woman, Have an Attitude

Secret fantasies
Living the unlivable life
Closed doors, shut windows
Slammed in my face
Operation subtraction
Shouting behind; at me
Fallen leaves, dry, cracked
    dreams
Love's reality

Be better than me—you have to
Forgotten hugs—wet kisses
A thawing hoarfrost bitten
    tongue
Inherit my knowledge
Stand up, sit down
I do love you
I do try
I have an attitude—

—Merina Wijaya, Grade 11

4. Write a poem about a fantasy or a daydream.

A Tropical Sunday Morning

Standing in church, I begin to daydream.
The priest's words fade away; I hear the muffled notes
Of a strange underwater instrument.
The stained glass windows blur, colors surround me
And form the shapes of umbrellas, cabanas, and chaise-
  lounges.
I am lying on a beach, tanned and warm.

I hear laughter on my right, and turn to see
A young family, three small children
Busy burying their father in the fine white sand.
Their mother looks on amused and concerned
With a small wrinkle in her forehead, and a thin smile
  on her lips.

On my left, a group of waders splash about in the sea
  foam and waves.
I decide to join them, and jog towards the ocean.
Walking into the water, my feet become heavier.
Unable to lift my arms and swim, I peacefully sink
Underneath the surface.
A school of yellow fish streams by my eyes on their way
  to a coral reef.
I squint, the fish blur, becoming a line of mass-goers as
  they parade up
the center aisle towards the altar for communion.

—Sabrina Comizzoli, Grade 12

5. Write a poem that fulfills a fantasy wish.

6. Write a poem that takes the form of a letter home from someplace
   away from home.

7. Make a poem that is a huge lie.

  I hunt
  I kill
  I eat small children
  Watch out.
  I am attracted to the scent
  of peanut butter.
  Know me by the smell of sneakers
  on my breath.
  I, the vulture.

—Kristen Dabrowski, Grade 11

8. Write a poem about a moment in which you changed.

Innocence

I've lost my blindfold.
Someone allowed the sun's undying
rays to touch my lips.
I can see the window, and there
appears to be something on the other side.
Beautiful yet strange, longing for a touch.
I long to touch them.
They do have names ... trees, flowers,
birds, buildings, cars, cities, states, countries,
the sky, the planets, stars, galaxies, the
vast universe....
The window allows me to see them, beautiful
and bright.
Alas, its glass and wood imprison me.
I draw the curtains back to hide it
from my view.
But it is there, a world which I cannot reach,
... my own.

—Ann Kim, Grade 10

9. Write a poem that expresses a mood you are in.

False Mirror

I look at it but do not see myself
I do not look as I feel
The image before me is not me but a girl
I am the spirit in the body that I see
A body is not a person, but a physical being
The person is the soul within the flesh
As I peer into the looking glass I do not see a
true vision—it's all just a false mirror.

—Katherine Kuser, Grade 10

10. Describe a good day or a bad day through one image from the day.

I escape slowly

from the still rocking screen door,
step from the warm wood porch
and into a light, unshaded wind that tosses
    glances at my hair and
    spins.

It revels in the luxury of one jewel:
    a cardinal,
I wish I could.

—Liadan O'Callaghan, Grade 10

11. Write an autobiographical poem, explaining either yourself or some experience of your life.

Song of Myself

The seed,
Cradled gently in the billowy breeze
Landing effortlessly on the yielding ground,
Shielded from the whirlwind;
Sprouting, budding, flourishing.

The blossom,
Swaying to and fro
Bowing to the compelling winds,
Disregarding the direction of the gales;
Submissive, timid, spineless.

The flower,
Erect with awakening
Resisting the gusts and blasts,
Tempest breaking its crispness;
Limp, wilted, dejected.

—Liliana Vargas, Grade 11

12. Describe yourself in a metaphor, as if you were some other creature.

I am the creature that cuts across the horizon
A fleeting glimpse for some
For others an ever-present dot against the crimson sun.
The bird that swoops when tired
But creeps again to new heights.
I am not the eagle
The majestic bird that glides ever powerful,
Roosting in distant cliffs; untouchable.
I am not the blue-bird
An angry one who is cold and blue like the diamond.
I am the humming bird
Perhaps not beautiful, but a happy being,
Never stopping until the work is done,
Always fluttering from the lily to the rose.

—Tara Grabowsky, Grade 11

13. Describe a feeling or moment in your life through metaphor or symbol.

The One Left with the Broken Heart

Do not expose this appliance to rain or
moisture,
To prevent fire or shock.
No trespassing.
Don't play with fire.

—Krystine Biesaga, Grade 10

14. Write in a stream of consciousness about any ideas that come into your head.

15. Write in a stream of images that follow from each other.

one doll that has not been hugged since I was 5

rainbow with no color lost in my painting of a flower found by the street leading to a place I do not know of one star remains painted on a country sky full of the color black like the darkness in a room where I can only hear the beating of your heart that has never been loved not even by the man in high school with whom you danced and kissed without love trapped behind a sturdy wall and mask covering it made of sheet lightning that no one even sees yesterday's tv stars in the microfilm room of the old large library with words that have never been read and the library is so quiet in the field except the crickets with a tear running down your cheek and the ticking but there is not a watch anywhere near by....

—Christina Jimenez, Grade 10

16. Write about a childhood memory (either a very clear one or a mysterious one).

Reality

5 am.
The temperature is below 32.
I step outside my garage,
and a funny thing happens.
It is dark and blue
and not a single sound can be heard.
Silence is big and heavy
I notice for the first time.
The busy road is deserted
The train station empty
No trucks, cars, or jeeps pass by.
I am being pulled back in time
where there are no words to describe
    the feeling
Everything is crystal clear.
I am incredulous
unable to believe what I see and hear.
There is nobody
yet I hesitate
to walk to the end of the driveway.

I run inside,
my shoes making a huge disturbance.
I grab my sister.
We walk slowly
and she giggles
Listen ...
She giggles some more
Maybe everyone is dead
and we're the only ones living ...
She makes her eyes big
and smiles uncertainly
Look at the stars ...
We aren't really seeing the stars,
but just the light they sent
billions of years ago ...
She says nothing
and still, no cars pass.

—Shuko Kawase, Grade 10

17. Images from dreams are vivid, strange, evocative, and often universal. Write a poem that includes dream images.

> As I stumbled into sleep,
> I was falling down, down
> a large flight of stairs
> When I hit bottom,
> books were flying everywhere,
> *Lord of the Flies, Frankenstein,*
> *The Outsiders,* and others pass by
> Lying on my bed
> No sheets
> "Don't Treat Me Bad" on the radio
> driving on the road
> no destination, no license
> Picking flowers with a little girl
> Get out of my small blue car
> I take a baby boy with me
> walking alone to my house
> sneaking in, not getting caught
> In jail, punching license plates
> Bright red nailpolish spills
> onto the floor and seeps inside
> my white jean shorts
> tripping into love.
>
> —Kathryn Calogredes, Grade 10

18. In a poem, describe your own birth. Or describe your own death.

A Taxi's Horn Blared

> A taxi's horn blared on W. 52nd—
> When I was born—
> The bustle on the street inched on
> Like the waves of the sea at growing tide—
>
> I breathed my first breath—
> Uttered a cry—
> Never before had earth heard me—
> A traffic light turned green—
>
> I stood on life's threshhold—
> The Wednesday rush hour began
> Another tire squealed—
> I was named.
>
> —Carin Companick, Grade 11

19. Write a reflective, meditative poem about an idea or a train of thought.

At Dawn
[written the day of Laura's grandfather's death]

Is there any meaning left
When you no longer exist
When no one calls you
By your name
Or even your gender
When they call you
"The Body"
What remains of you
In this world
Or rather
What has left "The Body"
If anything
Is there just a black abyss
Where you float for eternity
Is there something beyond this
    world
Something many people
Claim to have seen

Or is there nothing
No colors
No feelings
No memories or remembrances
Just nothing
I cannot comprehend
The latter
But until my time comes
I shall fear that
Nothing is out there ...

Perhaps I already knew
You were gone this morning
Before the phone call
When I woke up
To a forlorn voice on the radio
Crooning, "I will remember you."

—Laura Fitton, Grade 10

20. Write about your family, including family portraits, memories of family moments, family history, family places, or family stories.

Nana

Her house always smells of the roast
    always cooking in the oven.
And applesauce, made fresh just hours before.
Pressed dresses
And spotless aprons,
Coupons filed and neat.
Nothing can stop her from doing it all
Her deafness is only a light shadow,
    but she can hide it well.

He's been gone for three years,
So she walks where she needs to go.
She can't hear the cars that whizz by,
    as she marches to the store
To buy apples and chocolate milk.

—Jennifer Garver, Grade 10

Grandmother

As the cold insulated truck
Crawled down the street,
We sat eating our frozen lemon-ices,
Cold as steel in winter, but pleasant,
cooling now, slipping onto my tongue
with one lick and gone in an instant.

She sat next to me on a folding lawn chair,
Stockings rolled to the ankle revealing
maps underneath.
Her cotton skirt pulled just above her knees,
Shirt unbuttoned ever so slightly,
To capture the still air.

Fingers bent like forgotten knotty trees,
But eyes as clear and round as mine.
With a knowing smile of what little girls want,
She said we could take a ride to the beach.

— Katherine Leahy, Grade 12

Summer

My father raises the garage door,
Oil penetrates—
The four-year-old girl, at the neighbors'
House, sings rhymes while jumping rope.
He can only hear her hum—
Inside the phone rings, my sister
Runs downstairs to answer it—
My mother's in the kitchen,
I hear her washing dishes—
The family's wood-paneled wagon
Sits in the driveway—
I stained the back seat with Dairy-
Queen ice cream two summers ago—
A dog is barking,
two blocks away—
Dusk approaches
The street lamps glow.

— Michelle Evaul, Grade 10

Hand Game

1.

pink and stunted,
her index finger, timid, touches
the solar plexus of the gargantuan
    palm.
father's hand, clean for sunday but in
    ordinary time
veiled in black grease,
in the pure light, pleated with age and
    abuse,
is gentle.
she jerks her finger away
his hand snaps shut.

2.

sunny sunday morning
under the glaring
crimson lapis emerald ochre
filtered through stained glass windows
    depicting
a passion.
the comatose congregation
stands sits kneels stands sits
and never sings.
father and daughter play the hand
    game.

3.

fearful of being trapped
she pulls away from the dangerous
    palm
before it registers her presence.
giggles erupt the first time
she is caught.
zombie eyes dart
with secret envy
through feigned choruses of amazing
    grace,
feeling wretched.

4.

their hand game is true.
she and he, loving simplicity in
    childlike distraction
unconscious
of the power
it emits.

—Sarah Taylor, Grade 12

Poems That Start in Special Events, Experiences, or Activities

1. Write about the month or season of the year.

November

Every November I'll think of you,
because I saw all the leaves falling in your eyes,
I could see flickers of red and yellow,
I could see them tumble from the blustery season,
I'm going to remember how I paid no attention to my dog
because for some reason—my new companion became more
lovable,
I'll remember November for every thing my friend you are
and the falling of the leaves will not sorrow me,
may I always be reminded of your radiance—
like those colors,
—beauty and innocence,
A November example

—Shelley Wollert, Grade 10

2. Write about the weather.

3. Describe a sports event.

4. Write about a moment in a family trip.

5. Write about a class trip or a field trip. (Take notes on the trip to preserve details.)

> The egret wades with his long legs through the water,
> The water moves smoothly with the strong wind,
> In the strong wind soars an osprey which dives down
> for food at the water's surface;
> The water's surface carries the reflection of the trees,
> The trees are changing their leaves for the new season,
> from green to hidden shades of gold;
> The golden sunlight gleams upon the pond;
> The pond is the center of life and survival for its many
> creatures.
> It is their mother,
> Mother earth continues her cycle without man.
>
> —Jennifer Seass, Grade 9

6. When you go to a concert, dance program, play, or art exhibit, write about what you see or what you feel.

Adieu

> The lights dim
> on every part
> of the stage.
> the curtains
> fall
> gracefully to the floor.
> the shadows
> of the players
> join the blanket
> of darkness.
> Applause.
>
> —Jane Lee-You, Grade 11

7. Write about special school events such as assemblies, school plays, or dances.

8. Write a poem celebrating a special event such as graduation.

9. Write about your favorite activities, things you like to do, or repeated pleasures.

August Afternoons

I love
August afternoons
Weighty with water
Heavy with hay
Dust descending from rafters
Sweat and smiles and
Laughter lazily drifting

— Catharine Hornby,
Grade 11

10. Respond in poetry to something that happens in class (an idea, a joke, someone's behavior).

11. Look in the newspaper for articles about odd or interesting subjects to write poems about.

Poems That Start in Observation

1. In your daily life, be a sponge, a blotter: Write down in your writer's notebook as many details as you can about things you see and hear around you.

2. Make any observation from your writer's notebook into a poem.

3. Write a poem describing a landscape.

Landscape I

Barren
with sun-dried roots and
scarce, pathetic green
leaves scurry, twist,
frolic sedately
a stiffening, haunting cold
The sun is setting behind
two skeleton trees like a
suspended, illuminated
Florida orange.
Amidst this far-reaching meadow
and ominous sky,
I quaver alone.

—Mamta Chugh, Grade 12

4. Take a walk around your neighborhood and observe details to put into a poem.

The Burg

A balmy night with

dazed cars double-parked
near empty curbs

limp sneakers lynched
on twisted telephone
wires

suburban strangers numbed
in the living rooms of
corner houses converted
into Italian restaurants.

On to friendlier streets.

— Carin Companick
Grade 11

5. Take a walk in a strange or new place and observe details to put into a poem.

The Lone Tennis Shoe

Two buildings bank the tar river.
Heat kisses my face—
Not a light peck but heavy passion.
The lone wire of civilization
Hangs over a strange calm.
Where are all the children who run in the street?
The deep red of the buildings reflects
In the black of the street.
A tree sprouts from the sidewalk.
How does it do that?
Is it the tree that grows in Brooklyn?
From the telephone string
Dangles comfortably, like a white-black crow,
The sneaker of dirty white.

— Christine Cho, Grade 12

6. Write a poem that starts from looking at a photograph from your own album.

7. Look at photographs of people you don't know in magazines and newspapers and write a poem about them.

8. Observe one actor or dancer in a play and write a poem with that person as the central figure (either from your point of view or from his or hers).

9. Collect images or phrases from TV to put together in a poem.

10. Write a poem about an object that has personal significance for you.

Dust at Twilight

A shell breaks the water at sunrise.
Listlessly the gray chamber opens,
And a goddess is born.

Nineteen mountain ranges sink to the far-away sea
As water runs through hills and brushes tender roots of
     growing plants
Then sinks deeper until it finds its angry mother herding
     her clam-children.

A clam dug up by a thin, red-faced youth
Crumbles despite the infinite care
Of gentle fingers and soft brushes.

A child grins and laughs sharply as he pulls up a clam.
He runs to his mother whose lips pull up
And whose mind wanders to shells of years ago.

A dusty box yields treasures of childhood:
A clam shell, chipped at one corner,
An old notebook,
Three stones.

Living at last, a clam clutches a rock
As the brine washes over
And the seaweed trails
Like a goddess's hair.

—Catharine Hornby, Grade 11

11. Write a poem about a random object or a collection of random objects. (Bring in objects to hand around or display in your room to start this off.)

12. Observe one painting closely when you go to an art gallery and write a poem based on your observation. Choose a work that attracts you or seems beautiful in some way, a work that appeals to you for its mystery or its perplexing nature or that seems to draw your attention for reasons you may not understand, or one that somehow disturbs you and makes you uncomfortable or uneasy, seems ugly, or repels you.

Stand in front of the work for at least five minutes, writing down everything you see: colors, light, shapes, spaces, movement, design; what
draws your attention; how your eyes move; the length and thickness of
the lines; what feelings or ideas the artwork arouses in you. Write a
poem, using some of the phrases you wrote down.

The Sleeping Gypsy

White beams cast soft shadows,
Colors blending into one.
A woman dreams peacefully,
While a lion breathes close by,
The gathering has dispersed,
A guitar stands at rest,
Sand dunes are once again peaceful.
Temperatures drop, drop, drop,
All turns silent.
The moon and sun trade places.

—Claire de Lignerolles, Grade 10

13. Do the same as in number 12 with sculpture. Walk around it; look at
how the spaces work as well as the form; notice light and shadow.

The Immortal Bird

Forest of Fir trees
Pine cones, fruit
Finches, fluttering
Lichen jade, growing
Spiny, Clumped, Blotchy,
    Molded
Seasons of death
Fall, Winter
Shadow's growth, hovers
Hammer Head pecking,
    breaking
Away Life

—Maggie Akers,
Grade 10

Lifeless

Bones of a Dinosaur, Structures of a
    dead tree,
Slabs of Ivory Aztecs where abouts
Destined to be found.
Sleeping like a baby, yet fighting in a
    war,
the reconstruction of a gun (not possible
    to be around)
Standing like a broken toothpick,
but its shadow revealing Bugs Bunny
    bowing to his god.
Destroyed,
    Destruction,
        Dead.

—Khadijah Muhammad, Grade 10

Poems That Start from Thinking About Other People

1. Draw a portrait in words of someone you know.

Grandmom

Quivering fingers intermittently
dot against her artificial pink lips
Chortles and giggles too loud to
all but her deafened ears
Gypsy beads jingle as she tries
to stir their plastic lifelessness
Very high heels nearly
topple her delicate frame
Hair aflame with peroxide
her eyes very green yet they see
She looks for acceptance and love.

—Kristen Dabrowski, Grade 12

2. Draw a portrait in words of someone you don't know.

Unstung

Your flame only hardens with age—

With fish strapped tactlessly over your dank, scraped
   shoulder,
and fresh honey in your braided blond tangle,
you shunned the bobolinks and
told the world to go to hell

Cut-off jeans and bandannas,
"Try and stop me!" you laughed with purging ease
No one could.

Not caring to giggle or sip,
You slapped backs,
played poker, drank whiskey,
and fought in your untamed, martyr-like way
and in rustic, famined streets,
You embalmed virtue into archives and eloquent memories
into humble, instinctive, midnight love

On a stray night, you sat in a dark room,
abandoned by all,
and cried in unstung bravery—

—Mamta Chugh, Grade 12

3. Write a persona poem, speaking in the voice of someone else.

4. Write a letter in poetry that you never wrote in prose:

    - a letter you wish you had written
    - a letter you wish you could write
    - a letter to someone who isn't here

As I Write ...

My pen drops
    -another absence replaces a breath—
I scrib
    -grasp, grope, no air—
ble on
    -white sheets hold, envelope you, black, red boils, crimson
    pre-death air hangs but stands before you laughing—
sheet of ... nothing ... no substance
    -only its vapor seeps in—
spreads itself through my
    -writing brain—
tortured pen mind ... I only think of my
    -merge with black—
safe cell: unaffected by you—oblivious I would say, if I knew
    :but yet converged,
    tracing shared thoughts in red ink stains that
    reflect your face.

        —Liadan O'Callaghan, Grade 10

- a letter explaining yourself
- a letter reaching out to someone
- a letter saying something you could never say before

For Those Who Should Have Known Better

I was always supposed to be the
smart one, the thin one,
the glamorous one—
the perfect one

Being that can be so hard,
YOU expected too much
YOU asked for too much and
i ...

i let you down
i was too fat for you, too
dumb for you, too plain
for you, too ordinary

i didn't know how to be what you
    want
so
i pretended i did

i acted and played out my part in
    your game
became your toy and felt what you
    told me
to feel and saw what you told me
    to see and
believed what you wanted me to
    believe.

but, when was i I?

        —Justine Schiro, Grade 11

- a letter to an ideal, someone you admire
- a letter to someone you never knew
- a letter to someone you've lost

To Mommom

You have been gone for six years
And three months.
I've finally learned that I can live
Without you,
But I want to see your face.
The others that I've talked to
Say they see you in their dreams,
And I have not, but why?
I talk to you in my dreams at
    night,
And picture you there by my side,
And I hate to say it, but it is true,
You never appear in my dreams.
So I ask one thing from you,
Tonight when I close my eyes,
And enter into sleep
Let me see you,
Let me touch you.
Won't you please come into my
    dreams tonight?

— Jill Jefferson, Grade 10

5. Write a poem addressed to a friend.

Description of a Special Evening in a Letter to a Friend

I remember ...
Canoe dipped ever so
lightly in perspiration,
closeness immeasurable,
swaying softly,
a comforting caress,
fingers running through
the short waves of hair,
closing my eyes if but a moment
to envision memory,
a quiet sign,
a tender first kiss.

— Jane Lee-You, Grade 11

6. Write a poem about a friend.

Poems That Start from a Given Topic

1. Write a poem that describes something through color.

Autumn Colors

It is the amber in the chestnut fire of the lemon saffron ginger, tainted emerald from the dark mahogany which roasted honey.

It is the traditional cherry in the natural envy which blocks ruby and burns cinnamon to a cranberry blush.

It is bleached green but artificially blond at the same time until the peach auburn reaches absolute ember and the electric sap with its golden candle glow kisses the melon on the sun and lets the moon trickle through the last passage before winter.

— Shuko Kawase, Grade 10

2. Write a poem that has the color blue in it. (The literary magazine staff at my school came up with this topic for a bulletin board contest.)

Blue: Numbers

This can't even offer the sun
No bold, no flaming, no orange in the sky
But a frosted rug
and shards of ice in the water

The tiles bite my sole
The chrome shows me a bitter face
Even a far off crow laughs
as I fumble in the too early darkness

For all this, the obtrusively cheery
steel and plastic clock
dragged me from my bliss
The bright blue numbers proclaimed
6:14, wake up! wake up!
Dear, stupid blue numbers,
Why?

—Aparna Chowdhury, Grade 12

Blue

The Topaz blue of the sea stays in my mind for ever.
Like a memory of love it haunts both my days and nights.
The jewels of my heart are blue.

Little Sapphires gleam in the warmth of the summer night.
During the day the brilliance of the sky covers the earth
like a blanket.

The innocence of a new born baby boy meets the world in
    blue.
A stunning diamond that is historically dangerous
was christened Hope.

It is part of our flag and the pride of our people.
It is known as a sign of sadness, yet in my mind it is too
beautiful to know despair.

—Regina Guerrero, Grade 11

3. Write a poem about peace. (This topic came from a required submission to a peace writing contest.)

Sail Me Pacific

A boat, tossed at dock,
Does not expect calm
   beyond harbor doors
Knows only the heaving
   through strangers' wakes
And avenging them all
   with its own.

The boat that departs
   still water
Faces inland first
And reconciles its port

Before seeking farther
   horizons
   So that
By its subtle inlet
Wakes may be quelled
And with its outward channel
   reaching far to river
The raging current
   may find new
   timepeace
   to drift by.

—Carin Companick, Grade 11

4. Write a poem about hands (a surprisingly evocative topic).

Senses

Hands floating past me
come apart
I sift through the fingers and palms
Finding memories
I can no longer hold

I've lost my feelers
They've torn off
Trying to grasp the sense of your caress
is hopeless
In this mess I can't find them

The broken hands circle
draw me in
slap, poke
tear through my restless mind
searching for their thoughts
lost in a jumble
of eyelashes and fingernail clippings.

—Clare Gardner, Grade 12

FINDING TOPICS
IN PUBLISHED POEMS

*There is no such thing, really, as an original
voice. We grow from imitations and, like
sponges, absorb and grow full of all the voices
we have loved.*

—Derek Walcott

Poetry itself is one of the best sources to inspire poetry writing. Some element of almost any poem you read will give you an idea for writing. Student writers benefit from imitating established poets. (Kenneth Koch and Kate Farrell's *Sleeping on the Wing* is an excellent resource for model writing assignments.)[1]

But using published poems as a source for writing doesn't mean only imitation. Sometimes the topic of a poem will excite an idea; sometimes one aspect of the form, something in the language, the music, or the imagery may inspire a poetic response. When you read poetry, keep in mind the possibility of deriving writing topics from it. Some suggestions for topics based on published poetry are given in the rest of this chapter.

The student poems that follow were written in response to assignments inspired by poetry the class was reading.

1. Students enjoy writing a parody or imitating the form of a poem.

Crew
(Homage to Emily Dickinson)

I like to see it leap the Lake--
And skim the Crests of Waves--
And stop to fuel its Oarsmen up--
Then effortlessly glide

Along the Paths of Joggers--
And distantly ignore
The Shouting of Plebeians--
And then a wind assail

To fit its Shell
Through arching Bridge
Streaming forward all the while
In splashing spraying thrust--
Then chase itself downstream

Gliding like an Arrow--
Then responsive to the Cox
Stop--sharply and precisely
At its own weathered Dock.

—Holly Light, Grade 11

My Clock Chamber
(Homage to the *Beowulf* Poet)

Hark!
When the skin is reborn
In the east, my window
fills with lively light—which leaps
Upon walls; Patterned
With tiny stripes
Those gentle walls calm
My tensed nerves, at the end
Of a worrisome week. In the west
the fire ball falls asleep.
That, too, I can view
From yet another screen
Looking out upon earth.
Choose my clock-chamber, to
    hear chirping
of early feathered creatures,
To sense the stillness of night.
In my clock chamber,
As each hour draws past
You will see and hear the changes
of TIME.

—Clea Rivera, Grade 10

Between Two "W"s Lies Carlos
(Homage to
William Carlos Williams)

the hidden shelves
of the

library where
no one

has ventured lies
the dust

in which sits
the missing

puzzle
piece.

—Jane Lee-You, Grade 11

Merina's Creed
(Homage to Walt Whitman)

And I know the manual of life is God's written word
And I know nature is God's reward to me
And I know the parental hand is the one I should take
And I know people are my brothers and sisters and we are
    all equal
And I know love is the reason for life
And I know I must use my life to bring the world to shelter
And I know I must respect what life hands out to me
And I know I must not only smile at an exploring babe, but
    offer open arms
And I know the possibilities are endless
And I know I must practice what I preach and explore
    others' sermons.
And I know God is the creator and God is the father
And I know the oldest stone to the newest tear is important
    in the life span of the world
And I know poetry is my soul singing to me
And I know that I know the missing link in the chain that
    holds down humanity.

—Merina Wijaya, Grade 11

2. After a class read Gerard Manley Hopkins's "Pied Beauty" I asked students to write poems "in praise of ..."[2]

My Praise Goes Out

To the lush green gems
That cascade in boughs and streams
Or trinkling waters and life forms small and curious.
To the fresh emeralds reaching forth,
Climbing barks and bursting through
Roots and woven debris.
To the new-life buds crisp and widening,
Reaching through the air and filling in
The light pockets.
The green canopies break and scatter, falling;
Parachuting to the ground and nestling for
        rebirth next year.

—Wistar Dean, Grade 11

3. You can ask students to write a poem beginning with a line from another poem.

A Poem Beginning with a Line by Henri Coulette

Where are the people as beautiful as poems,
As calm as mirrors?
Perhaps in a place where all movements
Are madrigals
In a land where beaming light can be touched,
Hand to face
A warm palette of color forms a blush,
But a parasol is not needed.
Through the wind, urgent voices waltz
        as blooming lips
Form wonder marks
Here, lithe bodies dance a ballet in
        cursive while apricot palms
Are upturned, toward infinity.

Reflections there can only be beautiful.

—Kristen Dabrowski, Grade 12

4. Reading some poems by Gertrude Stein[3] or Edith Sitwell's "Facade"[4] inspires poems based on sound. I asked my class to bring in a list of words from a single category (mythology, geographical names, planets, and so on). We listed all the words on the board and then wrote poems that played with the sounds of the words.

Berries

Cranberry Thanksgivings
to eat sweet, summer strawberries
but not poison, boysen
berries
Birds eat mulberries
purple droppings
Purple, Black, and Blue berries?
or black 'n' blue berries?

—Elizabeth Moxon, Grade 12

5. After reading Walt Whitman's *Song of Myself*, I always ask students to write their own self-portrait in any poetic form.[5]

Song of Myself

I have been asked often
which nese I am
Japanese?
or Chinese?
foolish asker,
how mistaken you are.
Two continents claim my genes
the homes of Van Gogh
and Kyung Wha Chung
are my own
I live at the confluence of the
Danube and the Yangtze
My blood runs proudly in the
Taedong and Rhine
windmills and pagodas
dikes and water paddies
Calvinism and Buddhism
color my past

My ancestors
Fished along the shores of the
Baltic and Yellow Seas
in straw hats and wooden shoes,
Founded ancient dynasties,
Invented windmills
My grandfather's Fathers
were yang ban
and farmers
My Grandfathers
were politicians and theologians
They hid Jews
and were shot by Communists
I am a melange of
European and Asian,
and you ask me
Which nese am I.

—Julie R. Leegwater-Kim, Grade 11

Song of Myself

I like walking in the rain
without an umbrella.
You never catch the terrible colds
your Mom always said you would
Passers-by puzzle my promenade
Proudly poised I pretend not to see the
    perplexed
Perchance my wide smile will
Persuade participation in a precipitation
    promenade.
Don't curse the drops
They'll tickle your face too
Give them a chance.
I want to (just for a moment,
        just to see how it feels)
take a walk on the wild side.
I've always been predictable
I've always lived on my street.
I've always had PB and J on wheat
    for lunch.

The receding tide leaves a ribbon of us
    on the hard sand,
Each calcium formation different.
No two of us are the same
People are like shells.

Walking, one catches your eye
Your pulse and pace quicken
The treasure retrieved,
Either a beautiful perfect shell
or an ordinary one that only
    sparked your attention
to be tossed in the surf,
An ordinary shell that is, at second
    glance, perfect,
An unusual one, not perfect but
    worth keeping.
Then there is the shell.
The Shell. One you rinse in surf
Carry home like a new mother
It goes in a lamp or on a bureau.
It's always there
Reminding you.

Out of adversity happiness comes
Is the glass half full or half empty?
Look for good.
It is there, waiting anxiously to be
    discovered
like a half-disguised shell.
I must be patient.
I will see it.

—Stephanie Truesdell, Grade 11

The following writing topics suggest ways in which you might structure assignments based on ideas from poetry you read.

1. From "The Book of Thel," William Blake[6]

Ah! Thel is like a watery bow, and like a parting cloud,
Like a reflection in a glass, like shadows in the water,
Like dreams of infants, like a smile upon an infant's face,
Like the dove's voice, like transient day, like music in the air.

Assignment: *Create a series of similes to describe some aspect of yourself, as Thel is describing her mortality. Take only one aspect, and try to see it in several different ways.*

2. From "The Book of Thel"

Why cannot the ear be closed to its own destruction?
Or the glistening eye to the poison of a smile?
Why are eyelids stored with arrows ready drawn,
Where a thousand fighting-men in ambush lie,
Or an eye of gifts and graces showering fruits and coined gold?
Why a tongue impressed with honey from every wind?
Why an ear, a whirlpool fierce to draw creations in?
Why a nostril wide inhaling terror, trembling, and affright?
Why a tender curb upon the youthful burning boy?
Why a little curtain of flesh on the bed of our desire?

Assignment: *Make a list of questions to ask about some perceived imperfections of life, society, or the human condition. Experiment with using figurative language and rich sounds.*

3. Poetry by Sappho[7]

Leave Krete and come to this holy temple
where the graceful grove of apple trees
circles an altar smoking with frank-
incense.

Here roses leave shadows on the ground
and cold springs babble through apple branches
where shuddering leaves pour down profound sleep.

In the meadow where horses graze
and wild flowers of spring blossom,
anise shoots fill the air with a-
roma.

And here, Aphrodite, pour
heavenly nectar into gold cups
and fill them gracefully with sud-
den joy.

Assignment: *Write a poem that invites someone to a place that is special in your mind. It may help to think of a particular person whom you would like to have with you at that place. Use as many persuasively appealing images as you can, keeping them quite simple; let the pictures do the inviting. If you want, experiment with form, trying Sappho's short last line and word division between lines 3 and 4.*

4.   "The Panther," Rainer Maria Rilke[8]

His gaze has from the passing back and forth of bars
become so tired, that it holds nothing more.
It seems to him there are a thousand bars
and behind a thousand bars no world.

The supple pace of powerful soft strides,
turning in the very smallest circle,
is like a dance of strength around a center
in which a mighty will stands numbed.

From time to time the curtain of the pupils
silently parts—. Then an image enters,
goes through the taut stillness of the limbs,
and is extinguished in the heart.

Assignment: *Observe something very closely, to see exactly what it is like; try to get inside it to see what is going on. Be both specific and very objective in your writing: Don't turn the observed object into yourself, but turn yourself into the object.*

5.   From "Proverbs of Hell," William Blake (This is a random sampling from Blake's "Proverbs," not the whole poem.)[9]

The road of excess leads to the palace of wisdom.
He whose face gives no light shall never become a star.
No bird soars too high if he soars with his own wings.
Excess of sorrow laughs, excess of joy weeps.
One thought fills immensity.
The bird a nest, the spider a web, man friendship.

Assignment: *Create a list of "wise sayings." They can be what you have found to be true in life, or the opposite of what you really think: Be the "devil's advocate" if you want.*

From The Selected Poetry of Rainer Maria Rilke by Rainer Maria Rilke, trans. by Stephen Mitchell. Copyright © 1982 by Stephen Mitchell. Reprinted by permission of Random House, Inc.

6. From *Song of Myself*, Walt Whitman[10]

I am he that walks with the tender and growing night,
I call to the earth and sea half-held by the night.

Press close bare-bosom'd night — press close magnetic nourishing night!
Night of south winds — night of the few large stars!
Still nodding night — mad naked summer night.
Smile O voluptuous cool-breath'd earth!
Earth of the slumbering and liquid trees!
Earth of departed sunset — earth of the mountains misty-topt!
Earth of the vitreous pour of the full moon just tinged with blue!
Earth of shine and dark mottling the tide of the river!
Earth of the limpid gray of clouds brighter and clearer for my sake!
Far-swooping elbow'd earth — rich apple-blossom'd earth!
Smile, for your lover comes.

Assignment: *Write a description of a night that captures a particular feeling through its images and adjectives. (It may help to think of a very specific night.) Move on, if you want, from describing the night to include the Earth. You may choose to begin "I am s/he" and model your writing on Whitman's form, using "Night of ... Earth of ... ," or choose your own form.*

7. From *Song of Myself*

I know I am solid and sound,
To me the converging objects of the universe perpetually flow,
All are written to me, and I must get what the writing means.

I know I am deathless,
I know this orbit of mine cannot be swept by a carpenter's compass,
I know I shall not pass like a child's carlacue cut with a burnt stick
    at night.

Assignment: *Write a list of things you "know" about yourself.*

8. From *Song of Myself*

Who goes there?
How is it I extract strength from the beef I eat?
What is a man anyhow? what am I? what are you?

Assignment: *Write a list of questions about life that you can't really answer but find interesting and important.*

9. From *Song of Myself*

I believe a leaf of grass is no less than the journey-work of the stars,
And the pismire is equally perfect, and a grain of sand, and the egg
    of the wren,
And the tree-toad is a chef-d'oeuvre for the highest,
And the running blackberry would adorn the parlors of heaven,
And the narrowest hinge in my hand puts to scorn all machinery,
And the cow crunching with depress'd head surpasses any statue,
And a mouse is miracle enough to stagger sextillions of infidels.

Assignment: *Write a list of things you believe, trying through a series of images to show the miracle of life.*

10. "The Tiger," William Blake[11]

Tiger, tiger, burning bright
In the forests of the night,
What immortal hand or eye
Could frame thy fearful symmetry?

In what distant deeps or skies
Burnt the fire of thine eyes?
On what wings dare he aspire?
What the hand dare seize the fire?

And what shoulder and what art
Could twist the sinews of thy heart?
And, when thy heart began to beat,
What dread hand and what dread feet?

What the hammer? what the chain?
In what furnace was thy brain?
What the anvil? what dread grasp
Dare its deadly terrors clasp?

When the stars threw down their spears
And watered heaven with their tears,
Did He smile His work to see?
Did He who made the lamb make thee?

Tiger, tiger, burning bright
In the forests of the night,
What immortal hand or eye
Dare frame thy fearful symmetry?

Assignment: *Write a poem that is primarily a list of questions. Experiment with repeating the first and last stanzas, with or without variation.*

NOTES

[1]Kenneth Koch and Kate Farrell. *Sleeping on the Wing*. New York: Vintage Books, 1982.

[2]Gerard Manley Hopkins's "Pied Beauty" may be found in Helen McDonnell, John Pfordresher, and Gladys V. Veidemanis, eds. *England in Literature*. Glenview, IL: Scott, Foresman, 1987.

[3]Poems by Gertrude Stein may be found in Koch and Farrell.

[4]Edith Sitwell's "Facade" may be found in Richard Ellman and Robert O'Clair, eds. *The Norton Anthology of Modern Poetry*. New York: W. W. Norton, 1973.

[5]Walt Whitman's *Song of Myself* may be found in George Perkins, Scully Bradley, Richmond C. Beatty, and E. Hudson Long, eds. *The American Tradition in Literature*. New York: Random House, 1985.

[6]William Blake's "The Book of Thel" may be found in *The Poems of William Blake*. London: Routledge & Kegan Paul, 1905.

[7]Poems by Sappho may be found in Aliki Barnstone and Willis Barnstone, eds. *A Book of Women Poets*. New York: Schocken Books, 1987.

[8]Rainer Maria Rilke's "The Panther" may be found in *The Selected Poetry of Rainer Maria Rilke*. New York: Random House, 1984.

[9]William Blake's "Proverbs of Hell" may be found in *The Poems of William Blake*.

[10]Walt Whitman's *Song of Myself* may be found in Perkins, Bradley, Beatty, and Long.

[11]William Blake's "The Tiger" may be found in William Blake, *Poems and Prophecies*. New York: Alfred A. Knopf, 1991.

7 Writing About Literature Through Poetry

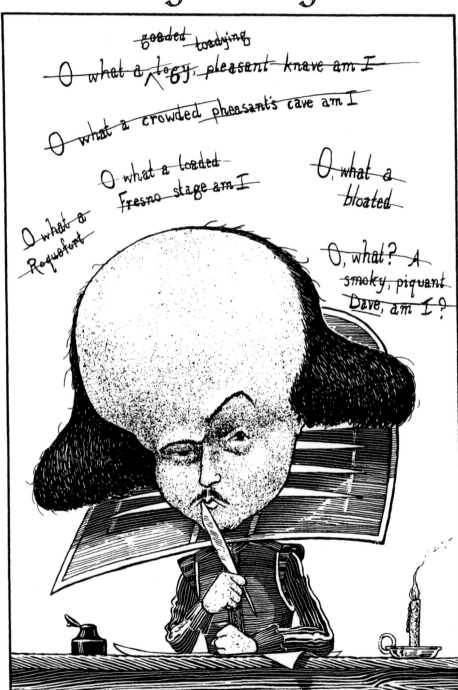

> The whole purport of literature, which is the
> notation of the heart.
>
> —Thornton Wilder
>
> Literature is news that STAYS news.
>
> —Ezra Pound

High school students are commonly asked to do expository writing of certain standard forms—description, definition, comparison/contrast, argumentation, persuasion, summary, and so on—often in formal literary analyses that focus on theme, character, settings, point of view, structure, imagery, symbolism, or tone in a literary work. "Creative writing" is put in a special category, frequently separated from reading assignments, and personal writing often is almost totally divorced from what the student reads.

Most English teachers chose to major in English because we loved literature. Our responses to literature were subtle and varied, ranging from intense personal reaction through the rational analysis of literary techniques. For us the pleasure of analysis grew from the pleasure we first felt in reading, what Helen Vendler calls "the response [we] can all feel to the human story told in compelling ways."[1] Critical analysis was certainly not our first response to reading; yet in a large number of English classes in both high school and college, students are asked to write about literature almost exclusively through analytical themes.

Even the most academically minded students sometimes find critical analysis a difficult and unnatural form of writing about literature. I don't suggest abandoning this kind of essay, but I do urge that we assign it as only one of a variety of possible responses to literature. In recent years, "reader response" has gained steadily in popularity as a method for students to write about literature; I see even more ways to extend the opportunities for writing about reading. Students will learn to write more naturally if, again, we can begin with the expressive or personal mode of writing and move casually both to the poetic and to the expository. Such movement allows students to be comfortable in their responses to literature and to write better because they are responding on two levels: the imaginative/intuitive/empathetic and the persuasive/analytical/reasoned.

WRITING LITERARY THEMES
IN POETRY

Standard topics for expository writing can easily be varied to allow students to respond to literature through poetry. Character analysis, for example, lends itself very well to poetic forms, many of which may open a character up from the inside rather than keeping the writer/analyzer outside the character. The following list suggests poetic ways of writing about character.

1. Write a persona poem, assuming the person and thoughts of a character from the work. The persona may be the protagonist, speaking in a
   moment of crisis or stress, showing inner feelings about an event, or in
   a moment of reflection, commenting on life circumstances, a philosophical view of life, or events in the work. A secondary character may
   speak, revealing something about the main character or indicating the
   importance of characters' interactions.

Untitled
(Persona Poem of "Offred" in
The Handmaid's Tale)

I can feel to the bone the heat of my
Red
Tent, pulling and jerking
My body into unknown contortions.
The women, foreign and strange to me
In their light clothes
Makeup
Stockings
T-Shirts
Heels.
I must endure this inexorable sweat.
The tent covers my body
And the white wings my eyes.
I cannot quite recall what it is to be so
Exposed.
Although now, I feel encumbered by my tent
It is another emptiness I cannot stand.
To them, I am a transparency.
An odd piece of history and culture as
They tour the city, taking
Pictures and trying to imagine
My life.
They will probably tell their children it is
Different.
It's okay, I will play the part;
I have been trained well. The aunts
Saw to that.
I lower my eyes—
No, my feet are still there.
In their flat practicalness
They haven't been anywhere the rest of me hasn't.
Don't you worry about me.
I will wear my plastic smile for you.
It is the only power I have left.

—Sarah Taylor, Grade 10

2. Write an interior monologue for one character, a stream of consciousness illuminating the state of mind of the character/speaker, such as the speaker in Robert Browning's "Soliloquy of the Spanish Cloister."[2]

**In the Eyes of
Susan Henchard Newson**

Life to me is but a sorry parade which
    I watch from the curb of some
    run-down street.
It has its good acts and its bad acts,
None of which I am a part of.
For I learned long ago that once you become
    devoted to something
    you depend on it.
And if it doesn't work out the way
    you planned,
You're the one who gets hurt.

So I just don't become involved in this
    parade.
Not emotionally or physically unless I
    know I won't get hurt.
I remain a bystander, which is much safer,
And in my opinion much more powerful
    than any single marcher
    there may be.

           —Anne-Marie Crowell, Grade 10

3. Write a dramatic monologue in which the character speaks to another person, revealing character through both what is said and what is hidden (as Browning does in "My Last Duchess").[3]

4. Compare and contrast characters by writing a dramatic dialogue between two characters from the work. Some poems that illustrate the dramatic dialogue are Robert Frost's "Home Burial," "The Death of the Hired Man," and "West-Running Brook."[4] Dialogues may be written by a single student or by two students writing collaboratively, each assuming one character's voice and viewpoint.

5. Write a character analysis in the form of poetic letters from one character to another. Elizabeth Barrett Browning's poetry is a good model for letters written in poetry;[5] Ezra Pound's "The River Merchant's Wife: A Letter"[6] is another superb example. Again, students might collaborate to write a series of letters between characters.

6. The standard character sketch may be written as a poetic description.

Miss Penniman

Decked in bugles, buttons and pins
She sits before her sewer's frame,
Her needle poised in hand, weaving her tapestry of fanciful
   life.
Sentimental work for an idle weaver.
Foolish thoughts, colored pink, dance through her mind.
Her lips tightly pursed, she embroiders her passions
For little secrets.
A pattern of contrived rendezvous with Morris repeats
   itself—
In the frame of church portals hovering
in an oyster bar.
Her largesse unlocks the Doctor's study.
Flowery speech she utters as confidante
to the few who will endure her.
Lavinia Penniman, a woman of sly temper, tender
   sentiment
and foolish romance.

—Holly Light, Grade 10

Morris Townsend

At first he seemed charming
That handsome Morris T.
Full of beautiful speech
And original ideas.
He did not enjoy books
Which fact would have offended
Any scholarly elder.
Rather, he wanted to view great vistas,
Watch dazzling actors,
Experience excitement.
Then his zest for life would be satisfied.
Morris T. could not work;
His relaxed nature delighted in
A sip of wine, a slow supper,
A chance to show himself off—
Life had to be a formal garden
For Morris T.

—Clea Rivera, Grade 10

7. For more unusual poetry writing about characters, imagine the character as an animal and describe its behavior and movements, or imagine the character as an inanimate object. (Ask the class first to list
   categories of inanimate objects, such as food, music, weather, and
   clothing.)

8. Invent a symbol for a character and describe the character in terms of the symbol.

9. Write a riddle poem that describes, without naming, a character.

10. Assuming the voice of a character, invent a song, a jingle, or a poetic slogan to sum up the character's views.

Other common topics for literary themes also may be written in poetry. The subtleties of narrative point of view, for example, can be as effectively learned by writing from different viewpoints as by formal analysis. The next group of suggestions focuses on writing about point of view.

1. Retell events of a work of literature from another character's viewpoint. Such retelling involves not only point of view but also narrative technique and character analysis.

2. Writing a "Rashomon"-type poem of several sections, in each of which a different character from a work describes a single event, person, or philosophical outlook, can be extremely revealing. Imagine, for example, Catherine, Dr. Sloper, Mrs. Penniman, Morris Townsend's sister, and Morris himself each describing Morris's actions in Henry James's *Washington Square*.

3. Working in writing groups, each student might take a different character from a work and write about a particular incident from that character's perspective. Make a collection of narratives, lyric poetry, or even a verse drama in which characters interact.

4. Write a poem about an event in a work from a perfectly objective point of view, then subjectively from a character's view, and then from your own point of view, expressing, for example, irony, sympathy, disgust, or admiration. You might add the author's point of view. This is also a good way to get at the significance of tone in literature.

This final list offers ideas for writing about setting. You can find similar ways to cover topics, such as symbolism, images, and theme.

1. Write a poem that describes the setting of a work.

2. Write a poem extending an author's setting by creating additional details that will maintain and underline the atmosphere the author established.

3. Write a haiku that captures the mood of a setting in a minimalist way.

CREATING LITERARY TOPICS
SUITABLE
FOR PROSE OR POETRY

Almost any of the traditional essay topics also make good subjects for poetry. As further suggestions for ways of dealing with literary topics and standard forms of writing through the poetic mode, I offer the following examples. The ideas I include here are based on *Beowulf*, *The Canterbury Tales*, *Brave New World*, and *1984*, chosen because they are some of the works I teach early in grade 10. I offer the lists only as models for assignments based on literature studied in the classroom. The same kinds of topics are very easy to develop for any piece of literature you teach, and through the assignment you can stress any literary aspect of the work you wish students to understand.

Most of these themes could be written either in prose or in poetry, or written first as prose and then creatively reimagined as poetry, or the other way around. They can all be approached in either the expository or the creative writing mode. For example, the assignment "Define the desirable qualities of the Anglo-Saxon king and hero; define the qualities of the antihero/monster/opponent" could be written as expository prose definitions of each of the types; it could be approached as poetry through a persona poem, an interior monologue, a dialogue, a poetic description of the types, or a narrative; or it could yield a short story or drama that defines the qualities through narrative and dialogue. The purpose of such assignments is to bring expository and poetic writing closer together, enabling students to use the whole range of the writing continuum in expressing their aesthetic, philosophical, moral, social, or personal responses to literature.

In addition to literary theme topics, I give students a number of specific notebook entry choices for writing about each piece of literature. The notebook entries are meant to encourage students to experiment with language and ideas in ways suggested by the work, to make autobiographical connections with their reading, or to learn special literary concepts (such as the kenning or alliteration). I also give related topics just for poetry writing, assignments that may ask students to imitate the work of literature or some of its poetic aspects, to encourage them to play with forms and to suggest new ways of self-expression.

Examples from
Anglo-Saxon Literature
(*Beowulf*, Anglo-Saxon riddles, "The Wanderer,"
"The Seafarer," the Venerable Bede)

The lists that follow offer suggestions for ways to deal with literary topics in prose or poetry.

Narrative

1. Retell the events of the epic (as many as are germane) in a monologue, assuming the persona of another character, e.g., Hrothgar, Unferth, Grendel.

Grendel to His Mother

Oh momma, momma, I'm just not a winner,
'Cause I got roughed up on my way to get dinner.
I shrithed to the Heorot to get human yummies
To tickle our palates and fill up our tummies.
The story I tell is both sad and perverse,
'Cause somehow my plan has worked in reverse.
I planned to kill Beowulf because I'm Cain's seed,
But he twisted my arm and left me to bleed.
When I bite the dust, Momma, please don't feel blue,
Think of it as a left-handed compliment to you.

—Kristen Dabrowski, Grade 10

Grendel

Tis true that I was born of the seed of Cain,
But I carry the curse by no will of my own
It is they who have bound me to my father's sin
Trapped me in a cage that my ancestors have wrought

It is indeed a shame that a land so great
Has become so base
Where a man is not judged for himself
But for the wrongdoings of his fathers instead

Yet have I to meet a man who can see past my ghoulish body
And my long, monstrous claws
The loyal thanes of Hrothgar have instead
Banished me from the fields of men

But they will not survive the passion they have instilled in me
They have enraged me as they have never angered any
    foreign king before
The bold thanes will pay dearly for their cruelty,
Blood will be shed over Hrothgar's Hall

My war-might will be known all through the land
I will make a name for the Children of Cain
Then I will make no effort to spare them

The mighty thanes of Hrothgar will perish at my hands
I will tear their bodies whilst they dream in sleep
They will not forget how they have ostracized me,
They will suffer for their sins as I have suffered for the sins
    of my fathers

—Aparna Chowdhury, Grade 10

2. Create a narrative of conflict between good and evil.

3. Write a narrative of a journey, which might be a physical, emotional, spiritual, or symbolic journey.

The Well-Read Traveler

The well-read traveler
Found surprises here.
A large city in the mountains,
She thought it would be
Alive with lights under a starry sky,
Streets filled with animated strollers.
The well-read traveler was wrong.
Hunger drove them
From their comfortable lodgings
Into an empty city.
Because she said there was a restaurant —
Fancy, elegant, and French.
Blank buildings stared at them.
No lights inside the window panes,
Like a ghost town.
Streets were swept so clean
Like a movie set.
The only other human in sight
Was a solitary policeman,
Standing at the curb.
Haywood Street?
He nodded down a couple of blocks
And eyed the strangers carefully.
Up and down Haywood Street they drove
Increasingly desperate
While the well-read traveler talked of
Delicate sauces, duck, and chefs.
The restaurant was a boarded-up building
Forlorn. "For Rent" said the sign.
No wonder the policeman thought them odd.
Backtracking through the spotless streets
They saw another misled family,
Dressed up, with determined looks upon their faces.
Probably all the doing
Of another well-read traveler.

—Clea Rivera, Grade 10

Description

1. Describe Grendel's lair or Hrothgar's mead-hall.

2. Describe one of those places as it would be seen by (1) a Danish thane and (2) a water monster.

3. Describe Beowulf's fight with the dragon.

4. Describe a place you know that reveals something about the character of its inhabitant(s).

5. Describe an experience of loneliness or isolation (real or invented).

Silence

No sign of life was visible in this
    white season
Crisp cold air seeped into my nostrils,
    chilling my lonely soul.
My gentle warm arms caressed one another
Down the narrow path of empty wilderness
No birds chirping.
Nothing
Stirred, except a dripping icicle beginning
to disintegrate.

           — Krystine Biesaga, Grade 10

6. Create a hero, heroine, or monster, using vivid language and images.

The Monster

It was a dark dingy day,
And the trees tipped towards the north.
We had always been told that when this happened,
The mad, malicious monster would appear.
And so he did at the sinking of the sun.
He was as massive as tyrannosaurus rex,
With four eyes of different colors.
A blue one that bubbled,
A red one like blood,
A green one shooting a laser beam,
And an orange one, glowing like fire.
He had no nose, and a toothless smile.
His muscles bulged through his matted gray hair.
He was disastrous, delirious, and destined to kill.
We feared him immensely.
He captured us and killed us.
He ate us after that.
He's finished, we're dead, it's over.

           — Jill Jefferson, Grade 10

Definition

1. By describing their activities, define the desirable qualities of the Anglo-Saxon king and hero; or define the qualities of the antihero/monster/opponent.

Always Behind

Desert, Forest, Grasslands.
Run for miles, miles, miles.
Up and down;
hill after hill
Always behind.
Never in front.
Always pouncing, putting me
    in new
situations.
Ugly, overwhelming,
obese, with ape-like features.
    HAIR.
Pounce fields.
Pounce forest.
Pounce nothing in sight.
Turn, and pounce.
Wave, current.
Never behind.
Always in front.

— Holly Gentempo, Grade 10

2. How do the characters of Hrothgar, Beowulf, and Grendel define good and evil by Anglo-Saxon standards?

3. How do the Anglo-Saxons define the nature of death in *Beowulf*, "The Wanderer," and "The Seafarer"?

Comparison and Contrast

1. Compare and contrast the mead-hall and Grendel's lair in as many ways as you can find, such as environment, physical details, occupants, and so on.

2. Compare and contrast *Beowulf* with "The Seafarer" or "The Wanderer." Consider mood and tone as well as content.

3. Compare and contrast Beowulf or Grendel with a contemporary hero or villain.

4. Imagine Grendel fighting Batman, or Beowulf and Superman getting together to fight for justice. Make up a dialogue, a newspaper account, or a diary entry.

Argumentation, Persuasion, Personal Opinion

1. Argue for or against a Christian author of *Beowulf*. Poetic: Be the author of the epic and talk about the events as you see them.

2. How did the Anglo-Saxons view nature? Include *Beowulf*, "The Seafarer," and "The Wanderer" in your thinking. Poetic: As an Anglo-Saxon or one of the characters, describe your thoughts about nature.

> During the early morning mists,
> The sea-mountains came rolling
> onto the beach.
> The soft sound was peacefully
> undisturbed.
> Sea-birds flew overhead, ocean-creatures
> swarm beneath the soft silent waves,
> The great fireball of heaven
> began to rise,
> Life began to appear.
> The new day was starting.
> Restless waves roared, fog began to fade
> and fall away,
> Water travelers carried people to and fro,
> And fish catchers began to throw out their nets
> into the open sea.
>
> —Jennifer Harris, Grade 10

3. Which is more influential in *Beowulf*, fate or free will? Poetic: In an Anglo-Saxon voice, describe your attitudes toward fate and your own destiny. In your own voice, compare your beliefs with the Anglo-Saxons'. In dialogue, argue the issue with an Anglo-Saxon.

4. How do you respond to the views of fate, life and death, or nature you have encountered in Anglo-Saxon writing? Poetic: Write a poem about your reaction or about your own thoughts on these topics.

5. At the end of the twentieth century, are we living in an age when heroism is neither possible nor appropriate? Poetic: Write a poem about late twentieth-century heroism or lack of heroism.

Dialogue

Any of these topics could be done by two students collaboratively, each taking one role.

1. Write a dialogue between Grendel and his mother before and after the battle with Beowulf.

2. Write a dialogue between thanes (Danish or Geatish or both together in the mead-hall).

3. Write a dialogue between any two or three characters from *Beowulf* or a dialogue among the Seafarer, the Wanderer, and any character from the epic.

4. Write a dialogue between two characters you invent to represent the forces of good and evil.

Oral History and Interview

Interview an older relative or neighbor: Who was his or her hero or heroine as a young person? Why? Poetic: Write the interview as a persona poem in the voice of the interviewed person or as a dialogue poem.

The next two lists show different kinds of writer's notebook topics you might develop.

Language Experimentation

1. Make a list of words to describe a monster, arranged under the headings "noun," "verb," "adjective," and "adverb." Then combine various words to create strong images.

2. Create a list of epithets that will give substance to a monster or hero.

3. Make a list of contemporary kennings, such as *idiot box*, *boob tube*, *couch potato*, and *lipstick*.

4. Invent at least six kennings to describe things you encounter in your daily life. It may help to start with a list of objects and then create a descriptive kenning for each. Try to go beyond concepts used by the Anglo-Saxons, such as "sun" or "ocean," and include articles from twentieth-century life, such as "radio" or "shower."

5. Practice alliteration. Start with pairs or triplets; how long a sentence can you make that is all alliterated?

Revenge ...

Waiting, wondering, wishing wildly—when would Willouby remember and return running?

Reminiscing, recollecting, recalling that wonderful wedding when Willouby, wicked Willouby, went waltzing out of my only offspring's overjoyous occasion ... the obnoxious oaf.

Outrageous ... overwhelming? No, not necessarily, not nearly as absurd as anxiety alienating a groom from his bride on the wedding day. He never came back, he left her there!

The bridegroom's betrayal of Benita, the bride, brings bitterness—but let bygones be bygones, right? Wrong! When Willouby, that Weasel, returns—redrum!

Murder! By me, her mother—my malevolence, malignance, maliciousness has made me mad, remorseless, relentless, retributive, retaliative, and ruthless.

Willouby's well-deserved end will come.

—Shonda Fentress, Grade 10

6. Create a metaphor for life like the bird from the Venerable Bede's story.

7. Create a series of images that show goodness or evil.

The Symphony

Then the silence ceased,
   a bell bonged.
From the statuette steeple a melodious
   tone sounded,
Harmony hummed through the hills.
As a tender-footed doe dances across a field,
A wild-haired rabbit rhythmically ran
   here and there.
Other animals participated in the piece.
A blue bird cried out with the carol.
The wind whistled musically,
And a continuous chorus accompanied
   the striking song
Until it abruptly halted,
For the conductor had ended its conversation.
At once, the lively performers
Became quiet creatures.

— Hillary Hurst, Grade 10

Autobiography

1. Generate a list of epithets for yourself like the epithets for characters in *Beowulf*.

2. Who is your hero or heroine? Why?

3. Write about a time you felt lost, isolated, alienated, or alone.

Barefoot

A child runs across the field.
The cold earth hits hard against
her feet.
Fog filters in the air, heavy with
mist.
She runs toward the rugged barn
house, yet cannot draw any
closer to it.
Faster she runs, no progress she makes.
She feels its warm interior,
she is cold.
Her legs are short, they do not provide
any speed.
She is lost in a barren field, barefoot.

— Michelle Evaul, Grade 10

4. Create a series of images that show loneliness. (Remember, show, don't tell.)

5. If you were to achieve fame, in what field would you want to achieve it? Why? Poetic: Imagine yourself having reached your goal.

The Game

They fought their way down the field,
Through obstacle and opponent.
Nothing could stop their trail to victory.
They dashed forward to drive the round treasure
Closer and closer to the white cage.
Streaking past straight lines into the shooting circle,
The defense on the end line.
The wing whipped the ball to the link,
Who settled, stopped, and shot it.
The sphere slid into the cage without disturbance,
A greatly needed goal accomplished.

—Stephanie Schragger, Grade 10

6. Write about a time you felt a "mission" to help someone else.

7. Write a "boast" (like Beowulf's description of his competition with Breca) about something in your life.

The following activities are designed to stimulate poetry writing.

1. Write at least twelve lines imitating Anglo-Saxon poetry, using alliteration and at least one kenning. Write about an event or a condition of your own life; another character; or a fairy tale, myth, or fable. Sports make good topics.

Chivas Regal

Striped tabby stalks on secret feet
    As silently as sunrise.
Delivers his delectable donation at my doorstep
    For me to discover.
A dead mouse, squashed,
    Limbs of lifeless ligaments.
Once a trustful and timorous rodent,
    Now a ravaged wreck.
My ferocious feline lurks
    Beneath the buried leaves,
grinning.

—Holly Light, Grade 10

2. Do some "mistranslation" of original Anglo-Saxon verse. (Give students a portion of *Beowulf*, Caedmon's "Hymn," or another poem in the original Anglo-Saxon and ask them to "translate.")[7]

Elaine
[from the Anglo-Saxon "Elene"][8]

She wears the chain of my heart,
Calm as easter weather. Perhaps clouds high.
Over geranium's glow under earth's fire,
Often my cloud beckons her to sleep, as I
Prance around under her room. Whatever I wear,
She seems saddened, without uttering a word,
And weeps beneath her hair, as I plead her to let
Me help by hiding without clinging to her.
Riding yonder to Ralph, my dying servant,
I camp without a need. Except the need to breathe.
Hurry and hide, help the unfound gold,
Old and weary. Weird was the night.
Yet early the horn was heard from the barn,
Which foretold, my much loved maiden had
    betrayed me once more.

—Claire de Lignerolles, Grade 10

3. Write an Anglo-Saxon riddle.

Grandfather

A grandfather built by a great-grandfather
Swirls of mahogany with mirrorlike shine
That spiral to the ceiling
Occasionally betrayed by worn spots
A large, golden, sunny face
The moon rising over its forehead
Marked by grooves of black
Gnarled, skinny hands
Counting off the minutes, tick
Hours, tock
At the very core of its aged body
Lies its heart
All in a row, suspended on fine chains
The burdens that bring life to this old man
Brass pinecones that inch up and down
As time flies
Needing an extra tug on the heartstrings
    once in a while
To keep him alive

—Rosamond Moxon, Grade 10
(Answer: a grandfather clock)

Riddle

When sun's flame scorched clear skies and grass
When buds and birds first bared themselves,
I hid you from both harm and heat,
My sea of fair green feather-fingers,
But close the sun with clouds and cool
You bring a blaze through blowing winds.

—Liadan O'Callaghan, Grade 10
(Answer: a tree)

4. Write a poem of place, using details that reveal the occupant of the place.

A House on the Lake

Drops of sunshine brighten
Dark, cool waters.
A man and his daughter
fish from a stained wooden deck.
Her pole—of blue, yellow and red
plastic.
She wears a red and white
checkered shirt with
navy blue pants and
little white sandals on
her feet
which dangle from
the splintery deck

—Amy Capotosta, Grade 11

5. Write a poem that retells, in modern language and free verse, the story of either the Wanderer or the Seafarer. Write in your own voice or that of someone you've encountered in reality or in books, movies, newspapers, songs, works of art, or plays.

6. Write a modern poem of a wanderer or seafarer in the twentieth century, about an incident or time in the person's life and what she or he has learned about life.

7. Go through your prose writings in this unit and turn one of those writings into a poem.

Examples from
The Canterbury Tales

The following lists suggest literary topics that may be written as prose or poetry.

Narrative/Description

1. Have a class version of *The Canterbury Tales*. The class first chooses a modern situation in which a miscellaneous group of people might be brought together for a certain period of time and decide to pass the time by telling stories. Then each member of the class creates a character and, in the third person, describes the character. Use details such as Chaucer's: physical characteristics (size, age, sex, facial features, clothing, and so on); personality or character traits (for example, good points, faults, faults disguised as virtues, amusing or disgusting behavior, way of talking); position in society; activities and interests (job, hobbies, other interests). Don't forget that tone of voice can make readers react to the character as you want them to.

   Write a story in the first-person point of view for your character to tell to the rest of the group. If you want, writing groups can get together to create groups of characters that will interact with each other. The prologues and tales may be done in either prose or poetry.

2. "How We Behaved That Evening." Chaucer says that he will tell how the pilgrims behaved, but he doesn't. Assume the point of view of one of the pilgrims (including Chaucer), or yourself in the role of a pilgrim, and describe what happens that evening at the Tabard Inn. What groups form? What do they do? What do they talk about? Are there any fights or flirtations?

"How We Behaved That Evening" poem follows on page 170.

How We Behaved That Evening

The narrator forgot to say
How we behaved at the end of the day.
He was jumping ahead to our tales, no doubt,
But here are the actions you wished to find out:
I, the high-schooler, and the cleric,
(Whose name, by the way, is Mr. Derek)
Would have studied from books for the rest of the night,
But he was intrigued by copyright,
(Which was printed in my books, not his,
And even if you're not a whiz,
You know it's a recent innovation)
So he left and sought the information.
In the meantime I was getting bored,
And so I, too, left and explored.
I ventured to the room next-door,
In which I heard the doctor's snore ...
As of yet I'd not secured
A room in which to be immured.
I thought perhaps the Wife of Bath
Would let me share with her. No wrath
She showed when I inquired,
But kindly did as I desired.
Little then, though, did I know
That she had no intent to go
To bed until she'd roamed around
The inn until she'd found
An eligible bachelor who'd
Sit with her and share her food
At table that night, at our dinner.
One could guess she'd grow no thinner,
For she would take her rightful share
(At least) from what sat ready there
Atop her trencher. She was forceful,
And with men (be sure!) resourceful ...

—Liadan O'Callaghan, Grade 10
[The poem continues, to describe actions of nearly
all the characters.]

3. Write a short tale or a fable in poetry or prose to illustrate a moral such as "Avarice is the root of all evil."

4. Choose one of the Canterbury pilgrims to describe in your own words.

5. Do a time travel either as a modern traveler seeing Chaucer's world from twentieth-century eyes or as a character from Chaucer's world seeing our age. In either case, try to describe what's strange, interesting, exciting, frightening, bizarre, and so on. Use images of as many senses as you can.

6. As yourself, or as one of the characters, write a letter home describing the pilgrimage and your fellow pilgrims.

7. Describe the Pardoner from the point of view of one of the "yokel minds" to whom he usually preaches. You may assume the persona of either an innocent who is taken in by his glibness or someone who is more knowing than the Pardoner thinks.

8. Describe someone you know from a Chaucerian perspective.

9. Describe a famous personality of today, using a Chaucerian manner and point of view.

10. Write about someone you know (personally or through books, movies, or TV) who is both outrageous and delightful, like the Wife of Bath.

11. Describe a character about whom you imply more than you say.

Cotton Picker

The plantation worker is a member of the black race,
one of the many faces of humanity.
In the fields, she picks the cotton clean
from its husks,
separating the downy white from the prickles.
All day she sings that God will purify her,
Although she will never be like the cotton,
she declares,
as the blood drips
from her blistered hands.
Cleaning the cotton, she sings
of the Last Great Cotton Picking Day.

—Jane Lee-You, Grade 11

Definition

For any of the following, a persona poem, dramatic or interior monologue, dialogue, or poem in which the narrator discusses the character in any way would be suitable as a poetic response.

1. Which of the pilgrims would you define as intellectual? (How do they fit the word: Can their intellectual qualities be defined in different ways?)

2. Which of the pilgrims would you define as crooks? How would they justify their dishonesty? How would you answer their justifications? How would others view them?

3. Which of the pilgrims would you define as heroic figures, if any? Why? What definition of heroism or heroic qualities are you assuming?

4. Define a modern stereotype by creating a character who fits it. Comment on that stereotype in any way you want.

Comparison and Contrast

For any of the following, a comparison/contrast poem might be written through dialogue or interior monologue or by contrasting symbols, metaphors, or imagery.

1. Compare and/or contrast the two women on the pilgrimage.

2. Compare and/or contrast a Canterbury pilgrim with a modern counterpart (a doctor, teacher, businesswoman, lawyer, nun, etc.).

3. Compare and/or contrast the Pardoner with a comparable charlatan from any age (and any medium, such as a contemporary or historical figure or a character from books, movies, TV, plays, or comic strips).

4. Compare and/or contrast the Wife of Bath with some contemporary woman, either someone you know or someone famous.

Argumentation, Persuasion, Personal Opinion

1. Take another text like the Pardoner's "Radix Malorum est Cupiditas" and write a sermon in prose or poetry to illustrate the text persuasively.

2. Argue either that Chaucer finds all his characters amusing or that there are some he despises. Poetic: Hold a dialogue with the author, or write a monologue in which he talks about the characters.

3. If the Wife of Bath were alive today, would she be a member of NOW (the National Organization for Women)? Argue for your position, writing from any point of view: yours, hers, a member of NOW, or another pilgrim's.

4. Who is the Old Man in the Pardoner's Tale? Argue for your point from the logical or the poetic point of view. Poetic: Write a dramatic or interior monologue.

5. What do you think women—or men—desire most? Describe it in prose or poetry; make it sound really desirable.

6. Write a personal reaction to any one of the characters.

Dialogue

1. Write a dialogue between any two to four characters.

2. Write a dialogue between yourself and Chaucer.

3. Write a "linking" dialogue between two or more characters and the teller of a tale read by the class, in which the pilgrims react to the tale.

4. Write a dialogue between the Wife of Bath and a pilgrim she is considering for husband number six.

5. Write a dialogue between the Pardoner and an "upcountry parson" in whose parish the Pardoner has been preaching (possibly even our Parson?).

Personal Writing or Autobiography

1. There was one character on the pilgrimage whom Chaucer neglected to describe: you. Supply the lack by describing this character as if Chaucer were describing you. You can be funny or serious, but remember to use details to describe this "character." Give the character a significant summary name: "The _____."

The Scientist

There was a young lady that rode along,
who sang a semi-phlegmatic song.
She had hair black as night down to her waist,
and researched information without any haste.
Her interest in science led to her profession.
She liked it very much, but it wasn't an obsession.
Happy she was and pensively she thought
to find the answer to the cure that she sought.
So on a pilgrimage is where she went
to ask God for the help to cure all men.

— Vanita Gupta, Grade 10

2. Write about a time when you joined a group in which you didn't know anyone. How did you feel about being an anonymous or new member? How did you handle the situation? In hindsight, would you have done anything differently?

3. Write your own "prologue" to a tale you would tell, in which you talk about yourself as the Pardoner and Wife of Bath do.

Oral History and Interviews

1. Interview an older relative, friend, or neighbor. Ask for a story from her or his youth. Write the story in that person's voice.

2. Interview any one of the pilgrims, as either (1) yourself trying to find out more about the character or (2) a television interviewer trying to reveal the pilgrim's characteristics to an audience.

3. In the voice of one of the pilgrims, interview yourself.

The next three lists offer ideas for entries in the writer's notebook.

Language Experimentation

1. Make a list of similes and metaphors describing the outward appearance of someone you know that would give hints about his or her personality (as in Chaucer's description of the Franklin: "White as a daisy petal was his beard ... it positively snowed with meat and drink ... his purse was white as morning milk").

2. Do the same thing as in number 1, about yourself.

Tara

I am a mirror, a sheet of murky glass
A pair of dusty glasses
I am the piece that doesn't
    fit in the puzzle
The top of a hill on a rollercoaster.
I am the comfortable jeans
    you hate to take off.
Most of all, I am the brief moment
before a firework explodes.

          —Tara Jones, Grade 10

3. Make a list of animal similes to describe a character (as in Chaucer's description of the Miller: "His beard, like any sow or fox, was red ... Red as the bristles in an old sow's ear").

4. List some traditional symbols of death. Invent some that a late twentieth-century person would understand.

5. Choose two or three adjectives to describe each of at least ten of the pilgrims. Don't repeat any of the adjectives.

6. Choose about ten pilgrims and say what color you see in relation to them. Tell why you see each color.

7. List some epigrams and apothegms (pointed maxims) from the Wife of Bath's prologue and tale.

8. List some epigrams and apothegms you hear going around in today's conversations.

9. Invent some epigrams and apothegms of your own.

10. Make a list of names that you think fit certain characteristics of people. Does your name fit your personality? If not, what name would you choose for yourself?

Understanding Character

1. Invent characteristics for a person to describe one of the four personality types or medieval "humors": melancholy, sanguine, choleric, and phlegmatic. Include physical details as well as behavior.

2. List well-known people from today to match as many pilgrims as you can.

3. Find pictures of at least five pilgrims in magazines or newspapers. Why does each picture look like the pilgrim to you?

4. List all the characters' names you learn. Do the names seem to fit the characters? Name the pilgrims who weren't named by Chaucer.

5. Write an entry from the diary of one of the pilgrims.

The following activities are designed to stimulate poetry writing.

1. Write some rhymed couplets to describe yourself and your friends; encapsulate the personality of each person in two lines.

2. Write a free verse poem describing a person (either real or fictional).

3. Write an Ogden Nash-style poem of rhymed couplets that pay no attention to rhythm.

Examples from a Unit on Utopias:
1984 *and* Brave New World

The lists that follow focus on ways of writing literary topics about the two novels.

Description

1. Create a mood through descriptive writing, as Aldous Huxley does in chapter 1, paragraph 2; chapter 2, paragraph 3; and chapter 3, paragraphs 16-19.

Drip

The old rusty sink stood alone Drip
The half vacant room Drip
Movement in the webs Drip
Like streamers hung around the room Drip
Dark and Dusty smell of fire and old Drip
Beat the metal drum Drip
Slimy and green it has formed Drip
Ear splitting sound Drip
Never ceasing DRIP
Heels of a woman walking away
DRIP DRIP Drip Drip Drip Drip Drip Drip Drip Drip

—Amy Hunter, Grade 12

2. Describe your own Room 101, in which your worst fear is used against you.

The Nightmare

Black,
all black.
Only walls,
no windows, no light
in this small enclosed space.
Nothingness surrounds me,
no sounds
except my screams,
which are not heard by anyone
    else.
Nothing to grasp,
nowhere to move.

Nothing to do except
sit
with my fists clenched,
my heart pounding,
my brow full of sweat,
and listen to screams
that won't come out of my throat.
I sit there
until everything is silent,
and I see nothing
but a white light.

—Vanita Gupta, Grade 10

That Night

A clear warm night
I can see the stars twinkle above.
My arms are tied down tight
Ropes holding my ankles are burning my skin.
The burning eased by a gentle breeze.
I hear an iron gate clang open
As soon as the ring of the iron gate stops in my ears,
I hear the clitter clatter of large hungry cockroaches.
I can't see them
They are coming from behind me.
The clitter clatter of the beetles grows louder
It sounds as if there are millions of them
I suddenly feel them in my hair and all over my body.
I still can't move
Tied to the ground, face up.
They cover me, crawling in my mouth and nose
Tickling my legs and arms
Biting harder and harder
And Blackness, I can't see anymore.

—Alma Moxon, Grade 10

3. Write one of Winston's diary entries describing his life in 1984.

4. Describe a place, creating a mood and suggesting the kind of life lived by the inhabitants, by describing a building, clothing, and food.

5. Take one characteristic of our society that you think is bad or dangerous and imagine it as the foundation of a new society of the future. Describe that future society.

6. Do the opposite from number 5: Take one characteristic of our society that you think is good or promising, and imagine it as the foundation of a new society.

7. Create a utopia. Include most of the following: philosophical basis, form of government, education, religion, the arts, media, family, social structure, work, entertainment, and recreation. If you want, include geography and climate.

8. Describe the last scene at John Savage's retreat as if you are a reporter, a "feelie" director, an average Beta, and Lenina.

Definition

1. Mrs. Parsons and Katharine seem totally shaped by the Party; Julia, though influenced, is struggling to be free. From what you know of the three women, define the "ideal Oceanian woman."

2. Define, from the viewpoints of the authorities in both *1984* and *Brave New World*, freedom, happiness, love, peace, and a stable society.

3. Define the terms in number 2 from your viewpoint.

4. Define the meaning and importance to you of any of the following: family life, religion, the arts, recreation, work, social life, or anything else you see misused in either of the two societies.

Mom's Kitchen

Smell of pot roast floats
   into my room.
My mouth starts to water
at the thought of the
hot carrots and buttery
   potatoes.

I picture my mom standing
in the kitchen with her
green quilted apron tied
around her waist.
She puts the finishing
touches on dinner and
calls my dad and me
to her wonderful meal.

—Danielle Vaughan, Grade 10

Comparison and Contrast

1. Compare and contrast Julia and Lenina as persons, as citizens, and as women.

2. Write a dialogue between two characters, one from each of the novels, in which they compare and contrast their societies: Lenina and Julia, Winston and the Savage, O'Brien and Mustapha Mond.

3. Write a dialogue between Winston Smith, Bernard Marx, and yourself about one or more of the following: views on death, ideas of love, notions of freedom, definitions of happiness.

Personal Writing or Autobiography

1. Which do you think is a more effective way to control people: through terror and coercion or through material satisfaction? Poetic: Show the effectiveness of either method through descriptive images, symbolism, or monologue.

2. Write about a time you felt like going against the majority (or established rules) and either did or didn't.

3. Picture yourself in either society, and write on one of the following ideas: What would you miss most from your own life? To whom would you be drawn or attracted?

4. Is individualism important to happiness? Express your own ideas about individualism versus responsibility to the group. Create a narrative to illustrate your ideas if you like. Poetic: Remember to show, not tell, your idea.

5. In either prose or poetry, respond to the idea contained in one of the following quotations.

   • "Reality exists in the human mind, and nowhere else.... What knowledge have we of anything, save through our own minds? Whatever happens in all minds, truly happens." (*1984*)

   • "You can't learn a science unless you know what it's all about. Whereas ... moral education ... ought never, in any circumstances, to be rational." (*Brave New World*)

   • "Stability. The primal and the ultimate need. Stability." (*Brave New World*)

   • "Perhaps one does not want to be loved so much as to be understood." (*1984*)

To Us—A Pair of Quacked Chics

In our pajamas at night
soaked from the sprinklers and
raising a ruckus.

11:30 tea time and late night snacks—
sesame sticks, Smucker's fudge,
We sat out on the deck
by the pool
and talked about life till
the sun came up.
We never got caught.

Putting the Mercedes in reverse
and rolling down the driveway—
At least Someone knew where
the brake was.

I think it was August
when we roamed the streets
of New York,
two tired, weary travellers—
A perfect picture for the photographer
at Rockefeller Center.
We were broke and
We were wet but
We were happy.

No one will forget when
we tied him up with
the nylon fishing thread and
left him in the basement.
We shouldn't laugh, but
we always do.

Another friendly "family get together"
As usual we went off in our own world,
speaking our secret language—
Who is it?
Who it is!
Frankly my dear, I don't give a damn.
No one understood us
then or now
No one except you and me.

—Asra Saleem, Grade 11

6. When John asks why beautiful literature such as Shakespeare is forbidden, Mustapha Mond replies, "Beauty's attractive, and we don't
want people attracted by old things. We want them to like new ones."
What is held up as "beautiful" by the people of the Brave New World?
How does that contrast with your definition of "beautiful"? Poetic:
Write about something you consider beautiful; write a persona poem in
which one of the characters discusses beauty; write a contrasting set of
two short lyric poems about something beautiful.

A Basket Full of Flowers

Picked on a Sunday afternoon
with the golden sun
gleaming brightly in a sky
of sapphire blue
the flowers
are as beautiful
as the carefully tended garden
of the old English estate
from which they came
and as young people
dressed elegantly
in clothes of white
enjoy a playful game of lawn tennis
the delicate pixies
in their bed of clean wicker
enjoy the delightful conversation
of afternoon tea
among the old ladies
in the garden.

—Paulette McKay, Grade 10

These ideas focus on activities for the writer's notebook.

1. Invent slogans that fit our society (such as "Community, Identity,
Stability" or "War is Peace, Freedom is Slavery, Ignorance is
Strength") to fit our society. Be satirical or serious.

2. Make up some hypnopoedic (sleep teaching) phrases that might be used
by the government of Oceania.

3. Make up some hypnopoedic phrases that might be used by our society
to convey "moral education." Be satirical or serious.

4. Write a paragraph in Newspeak.

5. List the names of people in Brave New World. Look the names up to
see how many of them refer to famous people from the past.

6. Invent at least five new people with names appropriate to the values of the Brave New World. Invent five people with names appropriate to the values of our society or to those of Oceania.

7. Think of a basis for the foundation of a society (as science and technology are the basis for *Brave New World*) and invent names for ten people to fit that society.

8. Write parodies of common sayings or nursery rhymes that could fit our society. Write some that could fit Oceania.

9. Write at least five new expressions for *Brave New World* based on folk expressions with which you are familiar (such as "A stitch in time saves nine").

10. For the humans in *Brave New World*, invent and describe a new athletic game that "uses up" materials and goods.

This list of poetry writing activities is based on *1984*.

1. Write a persona poem in which one character from the novel describes life in the society, talks about other people, or makes a political statement.

2. Write a poem about a fear.

Kidneys

im nervous
    im going to die
    everyone's angry at me

                stripping me
            throwing something white on me
im having a tantrum

        shakingscreamingcrying
    fear of the unknown

           is a great force
    im going to die
a bright light

                something red
    moving on a screen
        a mask
silence

—Laura Fitton, Grade 10

3. Write a dream poem using images from a beautiful dream. They may come from a real dream, or you may invent them.

Hidden Eyes

Hidden eyes.
They stare at me when I'm not looking.
But who's watching?
In the empire of the mirrors of light,
Everything comes out right at me,
Flowing into each other —
In those hidden eyes I see true visions of a
    bouquet of flowers —
Coral pink and pastel flowers so serene I
    can hear peacefulness
Dancing in the spring.

—Mai Abdala, Grade 10

4. Write a nightmare poem in which you invent a nightmare full of terrifying images or use images from a nightmare you have had.

Once Again

As I drive off into sleep,
I know that I am once again on the road,
And with me is my dying sister.
The lion pounces on her,
After devouring my kittens,
The lamplight turns red.
But I continue, hearing sirens,
Brakes broken,
A cliff in the distance,
My mother and father at the opeia,
Blackout in Minneapolis,
They head home.
Closer and closer approaches the cliff,
I scream,
Slowly I see myself in the mirror opposite
    my bed,
And with opened eyes,
I sit bewildered in the darkness of my
    room.

—Claire de Lignerolles, Grade 10

5. Write a poem about a childhood memory that is vague to you but about which you may have a strong emotion. Keep the vagueness and a sense of mystery about the memory; don't try to clarify it.

Vagueness of Childhood

Don't move down anymore,
the High Heels might see you,
the edge of the carpet isn't allowed to be turned up,
the perfume cloud suffocates me,
I could have fallen forever
if I tried to peek around the third stair,
as the laughter paraded downstairs,
the silence surrounded the contrary,
Sherlock Holmes, a two-year-old, and the loneliest
all in the same night

—Shelley Wollert, Grade 10

6. Take an object in your life that has a symbolic meaning for you (as the paperweight does for Winston) and write a poem about that object. Don't tell what the object symbolizes: Describe it or your reactions to it, what you do with it, where it is, and so on.

These poetry writing activities are based on *Brave New World*.

1. Write a "poem of propaganda" that teaches a lesson, based on a brief poem or advertising jingle with which you are familiar. Use as a model the rhyme in chapter 12, if you want.

2. Write a poem on one of the following topics.

- time

- the causes of happiness

- the important things in life

- the importance of nature

- family

Everyday

riding on a red bicycle
with my legs hung over the bar
and the big white hat I used to wear
in case I fell.
Up this narrow sidewalk
to get an italian ice, cherry
everyday
and my father and I singing
Ida won't you blow your horn
someone's in the kitchen with Dinah
The store seemed so far away
It really was only down the block
past the barbershop where I got my
first haircut ...

—Christina Jimenez, Grade 10

3. Bernard says, "Did you ever feel as though you had something inside you that was only waiting for you to give it a chance to come out?" Write a poem describing that feeling.

4. For the society of the Brave New World, or for Oceania, or for now, write a parody of a well-known song (in the style of "Bottle of Mine").

NOTES

[1]Helen Vendler. "What We Have Loved," in J. Engell and D. Perkins, eds. *Teaching Literature: What Is Needed Now*. Cambridge, MA: Harvard University Press, 1988, 16.

[2]Robert Browning's "Soliloquy of the Spanish Cloister" may be found in Helen McDonnell, John Pfordresher, and Gladys V. Veidemanis, eds. *England in Literature*. Glenview, IL: Scott, Foresman, 1987.

[3]Robert Browning's "My Last Duchess" may be found in ibid.

[4]Poems by Robert Frost may be found in ibid.

[5]Poems by Elizabeth Barrett Browning may be found in ibid.

[6]Ezra Pound's "The River Merchant's Wife: A Letter" may be found in X. J. Kennedy, ed. *An Introduction to Poetry*. Boston: Little, Brown, 1971.

[7]Caedmon's "Hymn" may be found in Samuel Moore and Thomas A. Knott. *The Elements of Old English*. Ann Arbor, MI: George Wahr Publishing, 1955.

[8]"Elene" may be found in ibid.

Glossary

adage — a saying that expresses a common observation.

alliteration — the repetition of initial consonants among nearby words. Example: "the furrow followed free."

allusion — a brief reference in a work of literature to a person, place, event, or another literary work.

apostrophe — a figure of speech in which the writer addresses a person or thing not literally listening or present. Example: "Death, be not proud."

apothegm — a short, pithy saying; an aphorism.

assonance — the repetition of vowel sounds among nearby words. Example: "Still hid in mist."

ballad — a narrative song or poem, a popular folk form. Ballads, which derive from the oral tradition, often use repetition and dialogue.

ballad stanza — traditional form for ballads, usually a four-line stanza in which lines 1 and 3 have four beats, and lines 2 and 4 have three beats and rhyme.

blank verse — unrhymed lines written in iambic pentameter.

cinquain — a five-line stanza, or a poem written in five lines.

cliché — an overused, trite expression or phrase. Example: "at break of day."

cluster — a form of freewriting in which a central word or phrase triggers associations, circling out around the key concept.

collaborative poem — a poem written by two or more people working together.

concrete poem — a poem in which the physical shape on the page represents the subject of the poem.

connotation — the implied and associated meanings around a word.

consonance — the repetition of sounds, particularly consonant sounds, within nearby words. Example: "It's still misty in the west."

couplet — a pair of lines in poetry, usually rhymed.

denotation—the definition of a word.

diamanté—a "diamond-shaped" poem of seven lines that are made up of, respectively: a noun, two adjectives, three verbs, a four-word phrase, three verbs, two adjectives, and a noun (either a synonym or antonym of the noun in line 1).

diction—the choice of words in a piece of writing or in speech.

dramatic monologue—a work in which the speaker talks aloud to an implied listener.

elegy—a serious, reflective poem, usually about death.

enjambment—carrying a grammatical unit over from one poetic line to the next without a pause or punctuation.

epigram—a terse, pithy saying.

epigraph—a quotation that appears at the beginning of a literary work to suggest the theme.

epistle—a letter.

epithet—a word or phrase used to characterize a person or thing. Example: "the white-armed goddess."

figurative language—language that departs from the usual denotations of the words, expressing one thing in terms that usually denote another; metaphorical language. Common figures of speech include metaphor, simile, personification, hyperbole, understatement, and apostrophe.

free verse—poetry that does not adhere to a specific pattern of rhythm or rhyme.

freewriting—writing intended to generate material by taking thought directly from mind to paper without interposing any editorial decisions.

graffiti paper—large sheets of paper attached to a wall for people to write on.

haiku—a traditional form in Japanese poetry that presents a strong image in three lines and few words. Most commonly, English haiku adhere to the pattern of five, seven, and five syllables.

heroic couplets—rhymed iambic pentameter couplets.

hyperbole—poetic exaggeration or overstatement. Example: "the very deep did rot."

iambic pentameter—a line of English poetry with five stresses of iambic pattern. Example: "The curfew tolls the knell of parting day."

image—a strong sensory impression presented through words.

imagery—sensations produced in the mind by language. The imagery of a poem includes both images and figurative language.

interior monologue—a work that projects the inner thoughts of the speaker and assumes no listener.

kenning—a metaphorical compound word found primarily in Anglo-Saxon poetry. Example: "whale-road" for "ocean."

limerick—a form of humorous poem, the limerick has five lines in anapestic rhythm. Lines 1, 2, and 5 contain three beats and rhyme, and lines 3 and 4 contain two beats and rhyme.

line break—a break in poetry, often without regard to sentences, where the author chooses to begin a new line.

looping—a series of freewritings in which the writer circles one word from a previous writing and begins a new freewriting with that word.

lyric poem—a song-like poem that usually expresses personal emotions.

metaphor—a figure of speech in which one thing is implicitly compared to another, without using the word *like* or *as*. Example: "Life's but a walking shadow."

meter—the formal rhythmic pattern of a line of poetry. The meter of a line of verse is determined by the pattern of stressed and unstressed syllables.

    metrical foot: combination of stressed and unstressed syllables that make up the metric unit of a line.

    common metrical feet:

        iambic: unstressed/stressed ("today")

        trochaic: stressed/unstressed ("wonder")

        anapestic: two unstressed/one stressed ("understand")

        dactylic: one stressed/two unstressed ("yesterday")

        spondee: a stressed single syllable ("now!")

metonymy—substitution of one thing for another closely associated with it. Example: "The White House said ..."

narrative poetry—poetry that tells a story.

objective correlative—an external object that suggests an emotion the writer wants to express without explicitly defining the emotion.

onomatopoeia—the use of words whose sound implies the meaning. Examples: *buzz, hum*.

oxymoron—a combination of contradictory words. Example: "sweet sorrow."

palindrome—a word or phrase that reads the same backward or forward. Examples: *kayak* or *Madam, I'm Adam*.

paradox—an apparently self-contradictory statement that has validity. Example: "I'm only cruel to be kind."

persona—a character fictitiously assumed by a writer as the narrative voice of a work.

persona poem—a poem in which the writer assumes the identity of another person and speaks in that person's voice.

personification—ascribing human feelings or characteristics to inanimate objects or to abstractions. Example: "The moon looks down."

personify—to ascribe human characteristics to a nonhuman thing.

point of view—the perspective of the person who narrates a work.

pun—a play on words, usually humorous, that suggests different meanings for words that have the same or similar sounds.

quatrain—a four-line stanza.

registers of diction—the language or areas of life from which the words of a work are taken.

rhyme—the repetition of a final vowel sound or final consonant sound preceded by the same vowel. Examples: "we-glee," "time-rhyme."
> masculine rhyme: single-syllable rhyme ("June-moon")
> feminine rhyme: multi-syllable rhyme ("honey-money," "syllable-fillable")
> off-rhyme, approximate or inexact rhyme: words that do not rhyme
>> exactly, but are very similar ("honey-loony," "brown-drawn")

rhythm—the metrical or rhythmic pattern of a line of poetry. *See* meter.

sestina—a complex form of poetry composed of six six-line stanzas in which the words at the ends of the first stanza's lines are repeated in a specific rotating pattern in the following stanzas, and a tercet containing all six repeated words.

simile—an explicit comparison between two things that uses the term *like* or *as*. Example: "My love is like a red, red rose."

sonnet—a poem of fourteen lines. Various traditional sonnet forms exist, with different set rhyme schemes. Traditionally, English sonnets are written in iambic pentameter.

stanza—a group of lines in poetry separated from other lines by a space.

stanza break—the place a poet chooses to move from one stanza to another, leaving a space to indicate the poetic unit.

stream of consciousness—the flow of thought in a person's mind, moving forward in time; in literature, the interior monologue.

stress—the emphasis put on a syllable.

symbol—an object or action that stands not only for itself but also for something more or something else. Examples: A flag is the symbol of a country; "to see the light" symbolizes understanding.

synecdoche—using part of a thing to stand for the whole of it. Example: "lend me a hand."

syntax—the order of words in a work; the way in which words are put together to form phrases, clauses, and sentences.

tanka—a form of poetry, adapted from Japanese, that expresses a mood through images and figures of speech. Tanka are five-line poems, usually with lines 1 and 3 being very short and lines 2, 4, and 5 somewhat longer.

tercet—a three-line stanza.

tone—the tone of voice of the speaker of a work, expressing the speaker's attitude toward the subject.

understatement—deliberate representation of something as much less in magnitude or importance than it really is.

verse—a unit in poetry. Verse can mean either a line of metrical writing or a stanza.

vignette—a short, descriptive literary sketch.

villanelle—a form of poetry with six stanzas—five tercets and one quatrain—in which the first and last lines of stanza 1 alternate as the last line of the next four stanzas and are repeated as the final two lines of the poem. The rhyme scheme is aba.

voice—the narrative point of view or the speaker of a work, which is not always the poet himself.

Annotated Bibliography

RESOURCES FOR TEACHING
POETRY WRITING

Behn, Robin, and Chase Twichell. *The Practice of Poetry*. New York: Harper-Collins, 1992. 299 pp.

Contains nearly 100 poetry-writing topics or exercises contributed by almost as many contemporary American poets who are also poetry teachers.

Bernays, Anne, and Pamela Painter. *What If?* New York: HarperCollins, 1991. 230 pp.

Although this book is subtitled "Writing Exercises for Fiction Writers," a large number of the exercises outlined here will give you good ideas for poetry writing as well.

Collom, Jack. *Moving Windows: Evaluating the Poetry Children Write*. New York: Teachers and Writers Collaborative, 1985. 180 pp.

More than evaluation is included in this book. It also has helpful suggestions for teaching children to write poetry. Aimed more at working with younger children, it still contains ideas of value to those who teach older students.

Gensler, Kinereth, and Nina Nyhard. *The Poetry Connection*. New York: Teachers and Writers Collaborative, 1978. 200 pp.

An introduction to using model poems as a source for student poetry writing. After a brief description of how to use poems as models for writing, the authors present ten ways to write poems (such as "Fantasies and Dreams" or "Persona Poems"), with suggested poems to use as models, followed by an anthology of poems by both adult and student poets.

Goldberg, Natalie. *Wild Mind: Living the Writer's Life*. New York: Bantam Books, 1990. 238 pp.

More writing ideas, both for warming-up exercises and for discovering sources of topics in the writer's mind and experiences of the world.

_____. *Writing Down the Bones: Freeing the Writer Within*. Boston: Shambhala Publications, 1986. 171 pp.

This book suggests ways to help students discover the individual voice and offers encouragements for the learning writer.

Gould, Jane. *The Writer in All of Us: Improving Your Writing Through Childhood Memories*. New York: Plume, 1991. 192 pp.

Using the writing process model, this book suggests many ways to tap into memory as a source for writing topics, and offers suggestions for revising and for working in writing groups.

Higginson, William, with Penny Harter. *The Haiku Handbook*. New York: McGraw-Hill, 1985. 323 pp.

Suggestions for how to use haiku to help students write poetry. The book describes the history and formal elements of haiku and includes tanka and other forms of traditional Japanese poetry as well. Useful for many age groups.

Koch, Kenneth. *Rose, Where Did You Get That Red?* New York: Vintage Books, 1974. 355 pp.

Koch, a leading American guru of teaching children to write poetry, argues for "Teaching Great Poetry to Children" and illustrates with ten lessons in which he had students from third to sixth grades read and write in imitation of John Donne, Wallace Stevens, Federico García Lorca, Arthur Rimbaud, and others. He follows with an anthology of great poems, including Chinese, Japanese, African, and Native American. Could be used at all grade levels.

Koch, Kenneth, and Kate Farrell. *Sleeping on the Wing*. New York: Vintage Books, 1982. 304 pp.

This anthology of modern poetry presents several poems by a number of authors, followed by a brief analysis of the writer's poetic vision and technique, with suggestions for writing on the model.

Macrorie, Ken. *Writing to Be Read*. Rochelle Park, NJ: Hayden Book Company, 1968. 278 pp.

A helpful and inspiriting book for writing teachers; full of assignments, exercises, and examples of student writing, as well as specific ways to teach the writing process. One chapter is devoted to writing poetry.

Rico, Gabriele Lusser. *Writing the Natural Way*. Los Angeles: J. P. Tarcher (distributed by Houghton Mifflin), 1983. 279 pp.

Subtitled "Using Right-Brain Techniques to Release Your Expressive Powers." The book outlines a method for generating ideas for writing and gives many assignments that could be used for poetry writing.

Ziegler, Alan. *The Writing Workshop, Vol. 1*. New York: Teachers and Writers Collaborative, 1981. 141 pp.

An excellent reference for practical suggestions about the writing process and how to organize and run a writing workshop in the classroom, along with suggestions about grading. One section is specifically about poetry writing.

_____. *The Writing Workshop, Vol. 2.* New York: Teachers and Writers Collaborative, 1984. 240 pp.

A book rich with ideas about assignments for expressive writing in both prose and poetry.

REFERENCE BOOKS ON POETIC FORM

Fussell, Paul. *Poetic Meter and Poetic Form*, rev. ed. New York: Random House, 1979. 188 pp.

Although Fussell defines the book as intended for readers, rather than writers, of poetry, the excellent discussions of metrics and of poetic structure are very enlightening for the poetry writing teacher.

Hall, Donald, ed. *Claims for Poetry.* Ann Arbor: University of Michigan Press, 1982. 498 pp.

A wonderful collection of essays on poetry by forty-three contemporary American poets. This is a good book to dip into frequently.

Hollander, John. *Rhyme's Reason.* New Haven, CT, and London: Yale University Press, 1981. 52 pp.

Hollander describes, writing in the form itself as illustration, the major poetic forms. Clever and instructive.

_____. *Vision and Resonance: Two Senses of Poetic Form.* New Haven, CT, and London: Yale University Press, 1985. 322 pp.

Fascinating essays on the music of poetry, metrics, rhyme, physical shape, and poetic language.

Padgett, Ron. *The Teachers and Writers Handbook of Poetic Forms.* New York: Teachers and Writers Collaborative, 1987. 213 pp.

A dictionary, with examples, of all the poetic forms you have ever heard of and some you may not have. It makes very interesting browsing as well as being a fine reference tool.

Preminger, Alex, ed. *The Princeton Handbook of Poetic Terms.* Princeton, NJ: Princeton University Press, 1986. 299 pp.

This detailed and scholarly dictionary of poetic terms includes definitions of forms of poetry and poetic elements, along with articles on such things as poetic theories, prosodic notation, and so on.

Index

Affective domain, 2
Ambiguity, 6-7
Ammons, A. R., 87, 96
Analogy, 11, 58
"Apparently with no surprise," 104
"The Applicant," 79
Arnim, Achim von, 4
Arnold, Matthew, 115
Audience—for poetry, 17, 23-26. *See also*
    Publication of student poetry;
    Writing groups
  in classroom, 17, 23
  local and national magazines, 25
  other schools, 25
  parents, 25
  in school, 23, 24, 25
Autobiographical writing
  in poetry, 123-33, 165-66, 173, 178-80
  in writer's notebook, 38-39, 44-46

Ballad, 96, 120
Bass, Madeline Tiger, 61
Baudelaire, Charles, 4
Beginnings and endings of poems, 101
  in revision, 107
Beowulf, 143, 167
  writing based on, 158-68
Bishop, Elizabeth, 87, 104
Blake, William, 146, 147, 148, 150
Blank verse, 99
Bly, Robert, 68, 87
"The Book of Thel," 146, 147
Brave New World, 158
  writing based on, 176-84
Britton, James, 3, 7
Brooks, Gwendolyn, 79, 98, 101, 104
Browning, Robert, 78, 104
Bruner, Jerome, 5, 6, 11
"Buffalo Bill's Defunct," 104
Bulletin board—as forum for publication,
  23, 28
Burnshaw, Stanley, 75

Caedmon, 167
The Canterbury Tales, 158
  writing based on, 169-75
"Cascadilla Falls," 87
Character. *See* Literary themes in poetry:
  writing about character
Class collections of student writing—as
  forum for publication, 23, 24, 28
Cliché, 29, 67, 71, 92
  lesson based on, 77-78
Clustering, 20, 106, 109
  illustration, 20
Cognitive skills—in curriculum, 2. *See
  also* Testing
Coleridge, Samuel Taylor, 7
Collaborative learning. *See* Writing groups
Collaborative poetry, 57, 73, 163-64. *See
  also* Writing groups
  in writer's block, 110
College admissions essays, 9, 10
College preparation, 9-10
Collom, Jack, 28
Computer link—as forum for publication,
  24, 25
Computers
  in poetry writing program, 22-23
  in revising, 22
  software programs, 23
Concrete poem, 96, 119
Connotation, 9, 10, 85, 87. *See also*
  Language
Contests—as forum for publication,
  24, 25
"Corson's Inlet," 96
Coulette, Henri, 144
Couplet
  heroic, 96
  rhymed, 99, 175
Crafting, 83. *See also* Revision
Creative thinking. *See also* Imagination:
  sparked by poetry; Intuition;
  Reason: and imagination
  and critical thinking, 4-5
  poetry's role in, 17

About the Author

Betty Bonham Lies graduated from Carleton College, attended the University of St. Andrews, Scotland, and received an M.A. from the University of Wisconsin. She was a 1988-89 Klingenstein Fellow at Teachers College, Columbia, where she began the work that resulted in this book. She has been awarded fellowships from the National Endowment for the Humanities to study at the University of Delaware, the Shakespeare Institute in Stratford-upon-Avon, Harvard University, and the National Humanities Center, as well as an independent study grant from the Council on Basic Education.

Ms. Lies has taught at the high school, middle school, and college levels in Michigan, Connecticut, Germany, and New Jersey, where for many years she has been a teacher and English department head at Stuart Country Day School in Princeton. She serves on the Geraldine R. Dodge Foundation Poetry Advisory Committee and the Professional Development Committee of the New Jersey Association of Independent Schools. A member of US 1 Poets Cooperative, she has published a number of poems and articles. She is the mother of two adult children and lives in New Jersey with her husband, Thomas A. Lies.